ORIGINAL
AUSTIN-HEALEY

ORIGINAL
AUSTIN-HEALEY

Anders Ditlev Clausager

Photography by Paul Debois · Edited by Mark Hughes

Published 1990 by Bay View Books Ltd
The Red House, 25-26 Bridgeland Street
Bideford, Devon EX39 2PZ

Reprinted 1991
Reprinted 1993
Reprinted 1994

Designed by Peter Laws

Typeset by Lens Typesetting, Bideford

ISBN 1 870979 13 3
Printed in Hong Kong

CONTENTS

Introduction

The photography is an integral part of the concept of this book. But it was also the hope to produce a sufficiently authoritative and detailed text, to satisfy the requirements of the Austin-Healey owner. Whether a newcomer to the marque or a long-standing enthusiast, whether restorer or concours entrant, Austin-Healey owners all seem to possess an unquenchable thirst for knowledge, about their individual cars and about the marque in general. To meet their expectatations, I undertook a lot of new research in preparation for this book.

It is my privilege to be the custodian of the invaluable original production records for most Austin-Healey cars, together with a collection of original factory technical and sales literature, found in the archive of the British Motor Industry Heritage Trust. I am sure that I speak for many Austin-Healey enthusiasts worldwide when I offer thanks to the Trust, and to the Rover Group, for their efforts in preserving this material, and for making it available.

It must now be accepted, of course, that when we look at cars which are at least 23 years old and in some cases more than 35 years old, it is quite simply impossible to be certain that these cars are in fact 100 per cent original. When the photography had been completed and the original draft typescript written, therefore, a number of Austin-Healey experts were gathered to look at the photographs and make their comments about the text.

The following were those who kindly agreed to attend this one-day seminar: Mike and Mel Ward (also the owners of one of the cars featured in the book); Keith Clapham (of BK Engineering, well-known Austin-Healey restorers); Gordon Pearce (100-Six and 3000 registrar of the Austin-Healey Club); John Wheatley (whose one-owner 1954 100 is featured in the book; as the former 100 registrar of the Austin-Healey Club, John has written two books of his own about the Big Healeys); David Jeffrey (of SC Austin-Healey Parts, one of the biggest spares suppliers in the UK); and finally, Reid Trummel, among the foremost American Austin-Healey experts, who put in what was very much a surprise appearance.

To have a panel of this calibre 'vet' the pictures and text was of immense benefit. They pointed out those small deviations from originality where they appear on the cars photographed for the book, and which have been highlighted in the text or picture captions. They also dutifully read the type-

There are times when it seems to me that I spend my entire working life – and have done so for these past ten years – dealing with Austin-Healey enquiries. Of course this is an exaggeration: in my professional capacity, as Archivist to the British Motor Industry Heritage Trust, I am as likely to be confronted with enquiries concerning almost any of the past products of what we know as Rover Group. But judging from the number of letters that arrive daily on my desk, Big Healeys are perennially popular, even after more than 20 years out of production. So although I handle Austin-Healey records every day, it has been a challenging task to write this book. The enthusiasm for these fine cars, and the store of knowledge that enthusiasts have been building up for so much longer than I have been involved, make me feel very aware of the position I now find myself in as the author of *Original Austin-Healey*.

Following the well-established formula for this series of books, a number of cars of the different models were located for photography through contacts primarily in the Austin-Healey Club. These cars had to be as near to their original specification as it is possible to find, and obviously also had to be in a condition suitable for photography. It is no coincidence that there are several concours winners from club events featured in these pages. Our photographer, Paul Debois, was then sent out with a brief to take overall pictures that would do justice to the chosen cars, as well as record shots of those minute details that mean so much to the Austin-Healey enthusiast – truly a case of every picture telling a story. I feel that Paul more than met these criteria, and the quality of his work featured in the following pages speaks for itself.

script, and I accept their corrections and amendments with thanks, not least because they were all so nice about it!

Apart from the mainly UK-based panel of experts, the typescript was also read by the following American Austin-Healey cognoscenti: Roger Moment (who has been instrumental in formulating concours regulations for the American Austin-Healey club); Bill Bolton (of the Oregon Austin-Healey Club, Bill also runs a register for the 3000 Mark II tri-carb cars); Rick Regan (who runs The Healey Den in Vancouver, Canada); and Hans Nohr (who runs Absolutely British II in California). Gentlemen, your additional input was of vital importance at a crucial stage in the production of this book.

However, despite the help and assistance which I was so freely given by all these people, I must stress that the responsibility for any mistakes which may be found in the finished book is mine alone.

The owners who very generously allowed their cars to be used for our photographic sessions were as follows: John Wheatley (100 BN1); Ron Walker (100 BN2); Peter Ellis (100M); Frank Sytner (100S); Roger Bakewell (100-Six BN4); Mike Ward (100-Six BN4); Roy Standley (3000 Mark I BN7); Alan Taylor (3000 Mark II BT7); Norman Pillinger (3000 Mark II BJ7 Convertible); and Ian Milne (3000 Mark III BJ8 Convertible). I should particularly like to thank John Wheatley and Roy Standley, both of whom I visited to look at their cars and make notes. Incidentally, I was delighted to meet Mrs Standley and learn that she is Donald Healey's granddaughter!

I would also like to thank Eddie Woods and *Classic and Sportscar* magazine (John Colley) who produced additional photographs of the BJ7 and 100S engine bays just when we thought we were going to have a problem – very much a last-minute rescue and all the more appreciated for this reason.

Last, but not least, my thanks are due to Charles Herridge and Mark Hughes, the publisher and editor respectively. The kind reception given to my previous volume in this series, *Original MG T-Series,* obviously encouraged them to ask me to tackle the subject of Austin-Healeys as well. I hope that I have not betrayed their confidence. Mark Hughes has, I fear, had quite as much work with this book as I have, but has been extremely patient and supportive throughout.

You will inevitably find that opinions dif-

fer where old cars are concerned, and it would be a brave man to claim that he had written the last word on any subject. At least I hope that this book will be of help to Austin-Healey enthusiasts, and I shall feel very flattered if it spurs someone on to do further research, even if they prove me wrong at the end of it!

Perhaps one explanatory word is required on the subject of nomenclature. I detest the use of the title '100-4' to describe the four-cylinder Austin-Healey 100, and I am equally unhappy about the title 'Mark IIA' for the Mark II Convertible or BJ7 model. Neither title was used at the time and I hope I have avoided them in the book, but I am aware that they have common currency. Some readers may be puzzled by my use of the title 'Mark II Convertible' but I hope this note will clarify exactly what I mean.

Finally I cannot resist quoting a passage

from a letter to me from one of my American readers, Hans Nohr, who obviously speaks from experience gained during a long and passionate relationship. I think he really says all that needs to be said: 'How did I ever get involved with these sweet, beastly, wonderful cars, anyway?'

Anders Ditlev Clausager
Birmingham, March 1990

Big Healeys Past and Present

Peter Ellis's BN1, which is even earlier than John Wheatley's car on the facing page, has been modified to 100M specification and also features rear reflectors. The Coronet Cream colour is unusual but authentic.

The Austin-Healey was the offspring of an unlikely match. On the one hand, Donald Healey's tiny concern at Warwick; on the other, one of Britain's leading car makers, the Austin company at Longbridge near Birmingham, dominated by the forceful personality of Leonard Lord. Another remarkable thing about the Austin-Healey: like few other cars, it was built with a single purpose in mind – that of achieving a dominant position in the American export market. It succeeded brilliantly.

Donald Healey, a Cornishman, had spent most of his working life in the motor industry of the Midlands. Before the war he had become chief engineer of Triumph in Coventry, where his most famous creation was the Alfa-inspired Dolomite straight-eight of 1934. He was an enthusiastic sportsman too, and was one of only two British drivers to win the Monte Carlo Rally before the Second World War. When the Triumph company went bankrupt,

ultimately to be taken over by Standard, Healey struck out on his own. He set up a company with a small factory at The Cape, Warwick, and in 1946 launched the first Healey car.

This used a Riley engine in Healey's own chassis design and was clad in aerodynamic bodywork. It attracted much favourable notice at the time, especially as for a short while it was the fastest production car made in Britain. Later Healeys came in a variety of models, some with Alvis engines, others built in collaboration with the American Nash company and using their engines. The Nash-Healey gave Donald a first impression of the requirements of the American marketplace.

Meanwhile, over at Austin, Leonard Lord had become obsessed with making cars for America. At this time exports for hard currency bulked large in the thoughts of every British motor manufacturer. The Austin A40 did quite well in America, and

in 1948 Lord introduced his A90 model, built especially with this market in mind, and called the Atlantic. It had styling to match and proved a disastrous flop – by 1952 it had faded away. Lord was by then exploring the manufacture of a small car for Nash, the Metropolitan. He also wanted a sports car to compete against the MG.

Three small companies prepared studies for a sports car that might satisfy Lord's requirements – Frazer-Nash, Jensen and Healey. The Healey 100, using the Austin A90 engine and sundry components in Healey's own chassis, and clothed in Gerry Coker's beautiful flowing bodywork, was a sensation of the 1952 Motor Show. Almost overnight Healey and Lord struck the deal that created the Austin-Healey. The car would be built at Longbridge, with Jensen at West Bromwich making the chassis and body assemblies.

Just 20 pre-production cars were made at Warwick before Longbridge production

got under way in May 1953. After a slow start, Longbridge rapidly got into its stride. Over a period of three years, production averaged over 400 cars per month, and at its height would reach almost 500 cars monthly. Just over 14,600 Austin-Healey 100s were made before the model was discontinued in July 1956 – about 10,000 of the original BN1 type with a three-speed gearbox, and some 4600 of the four-speed BN2 type introduced in August 1955.

It seems likely that almost 80 per cent of the production found willing buyers in the USA. By contrast, around 5 per cent stayed at home, the balance going to a great multitude of export markets where Austin was represented and known, even if Healey had not been. In commercial terms the car was an outstanding success.

It also began to make a name for itself in motor sport, Austin-Healeys beginning to appear on the race tracks and in rallies. Demands for higher performance versions

The early 1954 BN1 in Healey Blue belonging to John Wheatley, an excellent example of the original 100, is all the more interesting for being a one-owner car from new.

The Healey shape is attractive from any angle! It should be immediately apparent that this is a 100S (right), as it has no rear bumper, a perspex windscreen, a wood-rim steering wheel and an external fuel filler. This is Frank Sytner's car, in White over Blue.

From the outside it is impossible to spot that Ron Walker's Spruce Green car is a BN2. Although fitted with a louvred bonnet as per the 100M, it is mechanically to standard specification.

led to the development of the Le Mans engine tuning and conversion kit, marketed in 1955-56 on the 100M model, apart from being available for after-market conversions. Then there was the even faster and more special 100S, of which only 55 were built, in the Warwick shop instead of at Longbridge.

By 1956, however, the Austin engineers got their hands on Donald Healey's baby. They were anxious to get rid of the anachronistic four-cylinder engine, and perhaps they listened too much to the contemporary equivalent of market research. The result was the 100-Six, with a tuned version of the new Austin Westminster's six-cylinder engine, and with two occasional rear seats added in the tonneau of the car. The car was never as well liked as it predecessor. Matters were improved a year later when the original gallery type cylinder head was replaced by the more powerful six-port type. Also in late 1957, production of the Big Healey was transferred from Longbridge to the MG factory at Abingdon, henceforward known as BMC's sports car factory.

The MG men, led by John Thornley and Syd Enever, coped well with this erstwhile rival being foisted on them. In fact, they rather took it to heart. The following year, 1958, saw the addition of a two-seater version of the 100-Six. After total production of some 15,400 100-Sixes of all types, Abingdon brought forth the Austin-

The Longbridge-built 100-Six BN4 owned by Roger Bakewell is finished in Ivory White and sports the optional factory hard top. The wire wheels were by now also an option.

Healey 3000 in 1959, major changes over the 100-Six including an engine bored out from 2.6- to 2.9-litres and the fitting of disc brakes on the front wheels. Both two- and four-seater models were available from the start of production.

The 3000 was the longest-lived and most successful of all the Big Healeys. Of the original Mark I models, 13,650 cars were made until early 1961. The Mark II, which differed primarily in having a more powerful engine with triple carburettors, notched up another 5450 sales. Then, in 1962, they decided to civilize this hairy-chested brute.

The Mark II Convertible (the BJ7, sometimes called the Mark IIA) had a snugger hood and wind-up windows. That it returned to two carburettors worried nobody as the engine was almost as powerful as the superseded three carb unit. However, little more than 6100 cars of this type were made before the final version of

the theme was introduced in early 1964. This was the Mark III Convertible, with its 150bhp engine and further civilization in the form of a re-modelled interior with a wood veneer facia. More than 17,700 cars of this type were made before the Big Healey bowed out at the end of 1967.

The 3000 also brought fresh laurels to the Austin-Healey name in motor sport. The BMC Competitions Department at Abingdon and Healey at Warwick divided the kingdom between them. Abingdon looked after the works rally cars, and Warwick prepared the race cars for Sebring and other events. The commercial success in America continued. In the case of the 3000 Mark III, for instance, no less than 87 per cent of production was to North American specification.

Neither Donald Stokes nor the BMC-Leyland merger in 1968 killed the Big Healey – by that time the decision had already been made. It was an American

Mike Ward's 100-Six is an Abingdon-built example, finished in Primrose Yellow. The centre crease in the bonnet is unique to the 100-Six, while the grille is the same as that of the 3000 Mark I.

Pacific Green is another of the less common colours, and the disc wheels, supposedly the 'standard' fitting, are quite rare too. This is an extremely low mileage 3000 Mark I two-seater BN7 (above) owned by Roy Standley.

This 1967 Mark III Convertible (right), a BJ8 'Phase IIa' model owned by Ian Milne, is a left-hand drive car re-imported from the USA, and is painted the very rare Metallic Golden Beige colour, with black trim and hood.

lawyer called Ralph Nader whose one-man crusade for safer, cleaner cars led to the US authorities adopting the first safety and emissions standards from 1 January 1968. BMC decided that it would be pointless to try to make the ageing design meet the new emissions standards and decided to drop the Healey.

The Healey family would have liked to continue developing the car. A few prototypes were built of a Healey 4000 – a widened 3000 with the 4-litre aluminium Rolls-Royce engine (fitted in the Vanden Plas Princess 4-litre R). BMC toyed with the idea of a badge-engineered Healey version of the new MGC, but Donald refused to sanction the use of his name on this car. While he went on to collaborate on the Jensen-Healey, the last Austin-Healey (the Sprite) lost the Healey name at the end of 1970.

As the vast majority of Austin-Healey cars were always sold in North America,

this was for a long time the centre for Healey enthusiasm. Towards the end of the eighties, however, with fluctuating exchange rates and different market conditions, many of the cars originally sold in the USA were coming back to the UK, or finding new homes in Europe or Australia. We may well end up with a more evenly distributed number of survivors worldwide.

Inevitably many new owners may not be so familiar with the cars as they would like to be. Hopefully the present volume will help to serve their needs, but it may also be of assistance to the long-standing Healey aficionado.

The appeal of the Big Healey is timeless. But in the chapters which follow, the cars will be examined in detail, always with an eye to establishing as far as is possible what they were originally like when they came out of the factories at Longbridge or Abingdon.

The 3000 Mark II had a new radiator grille with vertical bars, shown here on Alan Taylor's four-seater BT7 model. Colorado Red over Ivory White was not a standard colour scheme and is not original on this concours-winning car, but a few cars were painted in this combination.

Norman Pillinger's Mark II Convertible, the BJ7 model, is correctly finished in Healey Blue over Ivory White, and has blue trim and hood to match.

Austin-Healey 100

CHASSIS

The chassis was a simple but effective design. Two parallel and straight box-section side members ran the length of the car. There was a dual crossmember in front of and below the radiator, connecting the supports for the front coil springs either side. Between the gearbox and the rear axle was an X-shaped cruciform structure. In the front angle of the 'X' was a short crossmember supporting the rear of the power unit, under the overdrive. Just after the centre of the 'X' were outriggers which provided mounting points for the forward ends of the rear springs. The rear ends of the springs were fitted to shackles on top of the rearmost crossmember, running under the petrol tank.

All the chassis frame members were square or rectangular in section. The main side members were 3½in deep by 3in wide, and were made up from two channel section halves welded together. The side members passed under the rear axle. From the front crossmember, rectangular tubes ran backwards and upwards at an angle to the bulkhead structure behind the engine. The bulkhead and scuttle was formed by a number of smaller sheet metal pressings, welded together and braced at the top. It was angled backwards at the rear. The vertical spaces on either side of the car were filled by triangular pieces forming the hinge pillars for the doors. The bulkhead incorporated footwells for driver and passenger.

There were two main body mounting points on each side, under the front and rear door pillars respectively. The floor was in two pieces, on each side of the propshaft. These floor panels were welded to the chassis and were bounded on the outside by the inner body sills. The chassis frame supported brackets for the front bumpers. There were three power unit mounting points, the rearmost under the overdrive as mentioned, and two front engine mounts, on each side at the front of the engine. On the outside of the right-hand side member, in front of the footwell, was a bracket of trapezoidal shape, supporting the brake master cylinder on a right-hand drive car. As the main side members terminated with the rearmost crossmember under the petrol tank, short channel section extensions ran backwards from the crossmember outriggers on either side of the petrol tank, to support the rear bumper brackets.

Because of the way in which the chassis

and body were constructed as one unit by Jensen, they were also painted together, and for this reason the chassis and the engine bay were the same colour as the body. The changes to the chassis during the 100's production run were minimal. However, very early cars had different front shock absorber mounting towers. The rear power unit mounting crossmember was changed early in production, at chassis number 140205, to accommodate a new type of overdrive. Similarly, there were small changes on the BN2 model (chassis 228047).

FRONT SUSPENSION

The front suspension was largely borrowed from the Austin A70/A90 range. It incorporated double wishbones and coil springs. There was an anti-roll bar attached to the lower wishbones, running across the very front of the chassis, and anchored to each sidemember. An extra stiff anti-roll bar was offered as a special fitting for racing. The upper wishbones acted directly on the shock absorbers which were Armstrong double-acting, type IS9/10R or IS9/10RXP. The castor angle was 1¾°, the camber angle 1° and the swivel pin inclination 6½°.

From chassis number 153855, stiffer shock absorbers were fitted. The shock absorbers were changed again at chassis 219137, to the co-axial type with larger valve chambers. At chassis 221404, the threads in the front suspension and fulcrum pin assemblies were changed from BSF to UNF. There were a number of changes on the BN2 model, from chassis 228047. The original R&M ball journal hub bearings were changed to Timken taper roller bearings. The front spring rates were

The front suspension and steering lay-out was little changed during the production run of the Big Healey, so this shot of John Wheatley's 100 is fairly representative. Our assembled experts had few reservations about the detail finish but did suggest that the inner pivot pin for the wishbone should be cadmium plated rather than painted. The nuts for the vertical anti-roll bar link should be the castellated type.

changed, and the free length of the spring was increased from 11.14in to 11.515in.

The front suspension grease nipple threads were changed from BSF to UNF at chassis 229626 (RHD) and 230078 (LHD). The final change occurred at chassis 230660 (RHD) and 230684 (LHD) when longer bolts were fitted to the coil spring seats. The actual suspension parts were painted black, and the shock absorbers were usually left in the natural silver-grey colour of the alloy used for the body castings but have been seen painted black.

REAR SUSPENSION

Conventional semi-elliptic springs were used for the rear suspension, again with Armstrong double-acting hydraulic shock absorbers (type DAS9R) mounted on the chassis side members ahead of the axle. There was an anti-sway bar or Panhard rod, anchored by a bracket by the left-hand spring bolts, and to the right-hand chassis side member.

Three different types of rear springs were employed. The first type of rear spring had a negative (laden) camber of ¼in (+/− ⅛in). From chassis number 148921, the springs were changed to a positive camber of ½in (+/− ⅛in) to improve ground clearance. Both these types of spring had seven leaves, with only the top (main) leaf wrapping around the shackle bolts. From chassis 152233 (intermittently) and from chassis 154647 (on all cars), stronger eight-leaf rear springs were fitted, with the two top leaves wrapped over the shackle bolts. This type of spring went back to the original negative camber of ¼in. There was a final modification to the rear springs when the hypoid rear axle was introduced at chassis 221536.

Other modifications to the rear suspension included altered rear axle bumper brackets to improve tyre clearance at chassis 146476. At chassis 220088, co-axial rear shock absorbers with larger valve chambers were fitted (compare the section on the front suspension). The rear spring shackle pin threads were changed from BSF to UNF at chassis 223220. There were no further modifications for the remainder of the production run.

STEERING

The conventional cam and peg steering gear was also borrowed from the existing Austin A70/A90 models. Originally, the steering gear was made by Burman, but from

The bracket on the right-hand side of the chassis supports the brake master cylinder on a RHD car, as seen here on Ron Walker's BN2 model. It will be noticed that the entire chassis and body unit is finished in the body colour.

With the centre armrest removed, the handbrake (here pulled on) is easier to see. The centre part of the propshaft tunnel may be removed. The carpet on the tunnel is original, the apparent difference in colour being caused by the fact that it is normally protected by the armrest whereas the carpet on the gearbox cover is exposed.

chassis number 230978 (RHD) and 231109 (LHD) a new type of steering gear box made by Cam Gears was introduced. On this type of steering box the diameter of the rocker shaft was increased. As the 100 was conceived with the American market in mind from the start, left-hand drive cars dominated in production; I would estimate that fewer than 10 per cent of the cars had right-hand drive.

The steering box was mounted in front of the radiator, with an immensely long steering column. On the early cars the column was adjustable, but from chassis 149930 a fixed steering column was introduced (corresponding body number was 1001 and an adjustable driver's seat was introduced at the same time). The Bluemels steering wheel was 16½in in diameter, with three equally-spaced wire spokes, with two pairs of wires each. The rim and hub were black. The hub carried a plain horn push in a chrome ring, and a self-cancelling trafficator (flasher) switch. The rim had finger grips on the reverse. When in the

straight-ahead position, the top spoke should be vertical (like a Mercedes-Benz star!).

The steering gear ratio was always 12.6 to 1, with about 2½ turns lock to lock. The turning circle was 35ft; track toe-in was ¹⁄₁₆in to ⅛in. From chassis 157624, the adjustable ball pins on the steering links were replaced by non-adjustable ones. Shim adjustment to the steering gear was replaced by screw-type rocker shaft adjustment from chassis 219137 (RHD) and 219258 (LHD). There were minor changes to the steering gear on the BN2 model, and an alternative design of steering tubes and levers came in with chassis 228932. The steering column, box and links were all painted black.

BRAKES

Girling hydraulically operated drum brakes were fitted, with 11in drums front and rear. The front brakes had two leading shoes. On RHD cars, the master cylinder was fitted on

This shows the correct silver finish for the brake drums and wheels. These are the original 48-spoke wheels.

the previously-mentioned outrigger bracket on the chassis, with the reservoir on the strut above. On LHD cars, the master cylinder was found on the vertical part of the engine mount, with the reservoir on the bulkhead behind the rear air filter. The handbrake was mechanical and operated on the rear wheels. The handbrake lever, positioned on the right-hand side of the propshaft tunnel, was the conventional as opposed to the fly-off type, and the lever and release button were chrome-plated. From chassis number 149903, the handbrake lever was modified to give better clearance to the tunnel.

Other changes affected the braking system. At chassis 156814, the brake pipe union threads were changed from ANF to UNF. At chassis 221404, the front brake cylinders were reduced in diameter from 1in to ⅞in to improve the front/rear brake balance. At chassis 221536, when the hypoid rear axle was introduced, the rear brake drums were widened from 1¾in to 2¼in, and there were also changes to the rear brake connections and the balance lever. The brake pedal was strengthened at chassis 222781, and the front brake pipes were modified at chassis 223136.

At chassis 227524, the front brake hose brackets were modified, and at chassis 227560 the rear flexible brake hoses were enclosed in spring steel armour to prevent chafing. On the BN2 model, from chassis 228047, the front brake drums were also widened from 1¾in to 2¼in. Where the early cars with narrow drums front and rear had a total friction area of the brake linings of 142 sq in, the friction area of the BN2 increased to 188 sq in.

The brake and clutch pedals rose vertically through the floor, and had rectangular pads (with a curved section when seen from the side) covered in studded rubber. The brake drums were painted silver. Alfin brake drums were quoted as an optional extra for the early cars with narrow drums. There were two types of Alfin drums: the original type had annular grooves around the circumference of the drum, whereas the later type had lateral fins on the drum circumference.

REAR AXLE

Two types of rear axle were found. The original type was the spiral bevel, ¾ floating axle also found on the A70/A90 models, with a final drive ratio of 8/33 (4.125 to 1). An alternative ratio of 9/33 (3.667 to 1) was optional. From chassis number 221536, it was replaced by a hypoid bevel, ¾ floating axle, of a new standardized BMC design, also found on the Austin A90 Six Westminster. The ratio of this axle was marginally higher, at 10/41 (4.1 to 1).

In either case, the axle was of the banjo type with a bolt-on differential carrier, and the axle assembly was painted black. The spiral bevel axle had BSF threads, the hypoid type had UNF threads. The rear hub threads were changed from BSF to UNF at chassis 222571. At chassis 228012, the oil filler plug was moved from the differential carrier to the rear of the axle casing. Also at this point, the rear hub lock nut threads became handed, with left- and right-hand threads, instead of both sides having right-hand threads.

WHEELS & TYRES

The original Healey 100 prototype of 1952 was fitted with A90-style disc wheels at first, but these were replaced by wire wheels and all 100s had wire wheels ever after. They were 4Jx15 centre-lock wire wheels made by Dunlop and each had 48 spokes – 16 long outer spokes and 32 short inner spokes. The wheels were normally painted silver, but a small number of cars were fitted with chrome-plated wheels – probably mainly for show purposes. The chrome-plated knock-ons did not carry any name or badge but merely the usual legends of 'left (near)side' and 'right (off)side', together with the word 'undo' and an arrow in the appropriate direction.

From chassis number 159802, the wheels were strengthened. The section of the hub was changed so the inner spokes could be straighter at the hub end. The gauge of the

The black brake drums are incorrect. It is not totally certain that whitewall tyres were fitted to any 100s as original equipment. As a matter of interest, these are Dunlop Road Speed RS5 tyres, a type introduced in 1960 on the 3000 model. The 100 would have had RS4 tyres.

rim material was increased from 13swg to 11swg. Still some owners are concerned about the risk of spokes breaking and prefer to fit the 60-spoke wheels from the late 3000 models. However, because these wheels have wider rims, they will fit only on early 100s with narrow brake drums. If fitted on a car with wide brake drums, these wider wheels will foul.

The tyres were Dunlop Road Speed 5.90-15, fitted with inner tubes. As these are no longer available, some cars run on radial tyres, size 165-15, others use 5.90-15 crossplies which are made by Avon among others, chiefly it seems for the VW Beetle.

While there were no further changes to the wheels or tyres during the production run, it is worth mentioning that the original wheel hammer with a hide head was changed at chassis 159257 to a lead hammer, which in turn was replaced by a copper hammer at chassis 229653. Similarly, the type of wheel jack was changed twice, at chassis 227339 and chassis 229080. Jacks were made by Shelley or King Dick.

ENGINE

A little history may be of interest here. Back in 1938, Austin's new managing director, Leonard Lord, decided to take Austin back into the truck market. He did so by producing a virtual copy, engine and all, of the contemporary Bedford, made by

General Motors in Britain. The Bedford engine, in turn, had been based on the Chevrolet 'Stove-Bolt' Six from 1929. During the Second World War, Austin was asked to produce a four-cylinder engine suitable for the planned British equivalent of the Jeep.

Two cylinders were simply taken off the truck engine to create a 2.2-litre four, which was first installed in the Austin 16 of 1945. That same engine went into the 1948 A70 model, as well as the Austin Taxi and several commercial vehicles. Also in 1948, a bored-out 2.6-litre version of this engine was fitted in the A90 Atlantic model, Austin's ill-fated early attempt at building a luxury convertible for the US market. It was the A90 Atlantic engine that Donald Healey took in 1952 as the motive power for his new sports car.

At 2660cc, it was one of the biggest four-cylinder engines available anywhere at the time, with a bore of 87.3mm and a classical thumping stroke of 111.1mm. With a compression ratio of 7.5 to 1, it developed a maximum of 90bhp at 4000rpm, with 144lb ft of torque at 2000rpm. High revving was not recommended; the limit was 4800rpm.

The architecture of the engine was conventional. Both the block and the cylinder head were made of cast iron. The forged crankshaft ran in three main bearings, of the thin wall, steel-backed white metal type. The side mounted

camshaft was driven by Duplex roller chain and also had three bearings. It activated the overhead valves via push-rods and rockers. The valves were vertical and set in-line, with double valve springs. The two inlet and three exhaust ports were on the left-hand side of the cylinder head, squeezed between the push-rods. The plugs, distributor, dynamo and starter motor, as well as the external oil filter, were on the right-hand side of the engine.

Pistons were of aluminium alloy, with three compression rings and a scraper ring. They had concave crowns. Inlet valves were 1.725in in diameter, and exhaust valves 1.415in. The valve timing was 5°/45°/40°/10°. Engine sump capacity was 11¾ imperial pints, with an extra 1¼ pints for the oil filter. The filter was a Tecalemit (FG2313 element) or a Purolator (MF26A element). From chassis/engine 213325 the filter was mounted vertically with a new adaptor. Normal oil pressure was 50-55lb at operating temperature, at 30mph.

The engine was painted 'steel dust grey'; in fact this was a metallic silver-grey-green colour which was always special to the Austin-Healey engines, and never seen on any other Austin or BMC car. The starter motor, dynamo, rocker cover and engine mountings were all in this colour. The engine paint has been reformulated and is available from specialists. Some early engines were painted blue.

The polished rocker cover is non-standard; the standard article was finished in the same steel dust grey as the engine. The air trunking in the background is a modern replacement; the original was black paper with wire stiffening. The air filters, black on this car, were painted steel dust grey on some later 100s. Note that the interior of the engine bay is also painted body colour.

The plug caps should have the leads coming straight out rather than at a 90-degree angle. Note the position of the engine number plate between the two centre plugs. The dynamo is correctly painted engine colour. The radiator hose should be fitted with wire clips, not the Jubilee clips seen here.

There was not a great deal of change to the engine during the production run, but a separate list of changes by engine number has been included at the end of this chapter. Details of engine tuning and the modified engines found in the 100M and 100S models will also be found separately.

COOLING SYSTEM

The cooling was assisted by a pump and fan, the latter with four blades, cast in aluminium and usually painted red. There was a thermostat in the water outlet of the cylinder head. Normally a 73°C thermostat was fitted, but cars supplied to cold climates were fitted with an 82°C thermostat. The cooling system was pressurised to 7lb/sq in, with an eared radiator cap. The radiator and header tank were painted black. The capacity of the cooling system was 20 imperial pints, and the normal running temperature was 180° to 195°F, the thermometer being marked in Fahrenheit.

A heater was fitted as standard on most 100s. This took its hot water from an outlet with a brass control valve on the cylinder head, returning the water to the water pump housing. The heater was made by Smiths and was mounted below the centre of the facia. Apart from the water valve under the bonnet, its only control was a rheostat switch for the built-in electric fan. The heater was usually omitted on cars exported to hot climates (typically Australia) but may also have been deleted on a few home market specification cars. The heater unit was finished in black crackle-finish paint.

EXHAUST SYSTEM

The three-branch exhaust manifold was left unpainted. It fed into a single downpipe, which incorporated a flexible section (improved from chassis number 149628). There was a single silencer mounted under the floor, literally just under the left-hand door. The silencer was made by Burgess. The tailpipe passed under the rear axle.

The exhaust system, which was painted black, was mounted at three points: at the front of the silencer, and two mounting points for the tailpipe.

CARBURETTORS AND FUEL SYSTEM

Austin cars had used Zenith carburettors for years. One imagines that it was only with the greatest reluctance that in 1948

As well as the heater finished correctly in crackle-black (but it has lost the Smiths badge, hence the blank area in the centre), this shot also shows the parcel shelf and the choke control. The fresh-air control is just out of sight to the right of the heater. The carpet on the bulkhead has been replaced but is still of the correct Karvel type.

It is difficult to see anything under a Big Healey unless it is on axle stands or on a ramp! But the flexible section of the exhaust pipe and the silencer, both painted correctly black, are just visible here.

they decided to fit SU carburettors on the high-performance Atlantic model, as the SUs were made by their dreaded rivals Nuffield! Anyway, the Austin-Healey 100 inherited its two SU carburettors from the Atlantic.

They were H4 1½in semi-downdraught carburettors with two-stud fixing. Originally needle type AH.2 was quoted, but from chassis number 148937 this was changed to a tapered needle, QW, for improved fuel economy. Each carburettor had a Burgess pancake type air filter, filled with oil-wetted mesh. The air filters were originally painted crackle black but changed to engine colour in 1955. The carburettor balance pipe was nickel-plated and the petrol pipe between the carburettor float chambers was in natural brass. Compared to the A90, the carburettors had slighty shorter dashpots to fit under the lower bonnet; they had hexagonal brass tops.

The rear-mounted fuel tank held 12 imperial gallons (about 54 litres) although larger tanks were available as optional extras (see list). The fuel tank was painted black and was placed on the floor of the boot, and was held in place by two black straps which were modified at chassis number 151608. The filler neck in the rear right-hand corner of the tank had a twist-lock chrome-plated cap. The fuel filler cap was inside the boot for security. The fuel pump was an electric SU high pressure pump, specification PP36. It was mounted behind the heelboard on the left-hand side of the car and was accessible once the left-hand rear wheel had been removed.

TRANSMISSION

The original Austin-Healey 100, the BN1 model, inherited its transmission from the A70/A90 models. This needs some explanation. These Austins had four-speed gearboxes with a steering column change. The Austin-Healey had a three-speed gearbox with a floor change. What happened was that although the original first gear was left intact inside the Austin-

Healey gearbox, the first gear selector was omitted and so the original second gear became first, etc.

Since this gearbox had been designed for a steering column change, it had side-mounted selectors, and therefore the Austin-Healey ended up with a gear lever mounted on the left-hand side of the transmission tunnel. The gearshift pattern was unusual. First was central and back; second was to the left and forward; third was back from second; and reverse was to the right and back.

The reason for abolishing the original first gear was that this was far too low for the much lighter and more powerful sports car. To compensate at the other end of the scale, the Healey was fitted with a Laycock de Normanville overdrive (bolted to the back of the gearbox) as standard. This operated on second and third speeds and was controlled by a switch on the facia. The net result was that the Healey driver had five speeds to play around with.

The clutch was a mechanically operated Borg & Beck single dry-plate type of 9in diameter. On the BN1, the clutch housing and gearbox were in one piece, and were mostly left in unpainted aluminium. One side effect of using a three-speed version of a

By contrast, the four-speed BN2 model has a much wider gearbox cover, with the gearlever on top, although still clearly off-set to the left. The carpet on this car has probably been replaced, and the armrest is also new, and so a different colour from the seat.

four-speed box was that all forward gears had synchromesh.

The most important change to the BN1 transmission came early in the production run, when the type of overdrive was changed from WN1260 (with a 32.4 per cent reduction) to WN1292 (with a 28.6 per cent reduction). This happened at chassis number 140205 as early as August 1953, which in effect means that only a handful of cars had the early type overdrive. A close-ratio overdrive (22 per cent reduction) was optional.

Allowing for the two different overdrive reduction ratios, and also for the subsequent change in final drive ratio when the hypoid axle was introduced, we get the following tables of internal and overall gear ratios:

INTERNAL RATIOS

	Early type overdrive	Later type overdrive
First	2.25	2.25
Second	1.42	1.42
Second o/d	1.07	1.105
Third	1.00	1.00
Third o/d	0.756	0.778
Reverse	4.97	4.97

OVERALL RATIOS

	Early type overdrive (s/b axle)	Later type overdrive (s/b axle)	Later type overdrive (hypoid axle)
First	9.28	9.28	9.22
Second	5.85	5.85	5.82
Second o/d	4.42	4.56	4.53
Third	4.125	4.125	4.1
Third o/d	3.12	3.21	3.19
Reverse	20.5	20.5	20.4

These tables do not take into account the alternative rear axle ratio of 3.66 to 1 quoted for the spiral bevel axle, but this would obviously affect the overall ratios quoted above, as would the optional close-ratio 22 per cent reduction overdrive.

The gearlever itself was chrome-plated and had a round black knob, with the pattern engraved in white. The lever had a moulded rubber gaiter at its foot, usually with a Vynide area inset in the carpet surrounding it. Because it was offset to the left, the gearlever on left-hand drive cars

was much shorter than on right-hand drive cars.

The biggest single modification on the BN2 model, from chassis number 228047 in August 1955, was the introduction of a new four-speed gearbox, with synchromesh on the upper three ratios. As the dual overdrive – now working on third and fourth speeds – was still fitted, there were now in effect six gears. The new gearbox was that of the recently-introduced Austin A90 Six Westminster model, and as it was still primarily designed for steering column change, the Austin-Healey gearlever remained off-centre. At least it now had a normal shift pattern – first in the centre and forward, second behind, third to the right and forward, fourth behind, and reverse on a dog leg to the left and back. The ratios were now as follows:

	INTERNAL RATIOS	OVERALL RATIOS
First	3.07	12.6
Second	1.91	7.85
Third	1.33	5.46
Third o/d	1.03	4.24
Fourth	1.00	4.1
Fourth o/d	0.778	3.18
Reverse	4.17	17.1

The overdrive itself was also modified on the BN2 model. Most importantly, there was now only one overdrive relay instead of the two relays found on the BN1, and the wiring was simplified. The overdrive reduction ratio was now 28 per cent. The type of overdrive was WN1308.

Originally, the BN2 cars used the same gearlever on right-hand and left-hand drive cars, but from chassis number 228487 the gearlever was modified, with two alternative types of gearlever being quoted for either right-hand or left-hand drive cars. The shape of the transmission tunnel was altered on the BN2 model, the tunnel being squarer in section, and the rubber gaiter for the gearlever was sunk below the level of the carpet. The edge of the carpet around the gearlever hole was bound in Vynide. Where the BN1 had a Vynide covered access panel for the gearbox oil filler on the right-hand side of the tunnel, the BN2 had a rubber plug for the combined dipstick and oil filler under the carpet at the front of the gearbox cover. Finally, it must be mentioned that on the BN2 there was a separate

aluminium clutch housing, and both this and the cast iron gearbox were now finished in engine paint colour.

The propshaft was of the open type, made by Hardy Spicer, with universal joints front and rear and always painted black. Originally the propshaft was 21⅛in long, but with the change in overdrive at chassis 140205 it was shortened to 20¾in. The bolts holding the propshaft coupling flange to the overdrive were changed at chassis 155284. With the coming of the hypoid rear axle at chassis 221536, the propshaft was further shortened to 20in.

Some further detail changes to the transmission have been listed in the table summarising change points at the end of this chapter.

ELECTRICAL EQUIPMENT AND LAMPS

The electrical equipment was supplied by Lucas. Two six-volt batteries were fitted, type SLTW11E, with a 50 AH capacity. The batteries were mounted on shelves on the chassis and were accessible through a trapdoor in the tonneau floor behind the seats. The batteries were connected in series and were wired positive to earth, via a battery master switch found in the boot. Some export cars were fitted with dry-charged batteries, but for certain destinations batteries may not have been fitted at all. The wiring had colour-coded cotton covering.

The dynamo was type C45PV5 and the starter motor type M418PG. Both were usually finished in the same colour as the engine, and so was the bracket for the dynamo. The distributor was type DM2P4, with automatic advance and retard. From chassis number 230361, pre-tilted contact breakers were fitted, and the Lucas part number was changed from 40320 to 40495. The distributor cap remained the same. The original ignition coil was type B12/1 but from chassis 225780 an oil-filled ignition coil type B.21 was fitted. The coil was black, and was attached to the side of the engine just behind the distributor. The sparking plugs were Champion NA.8 14mm long reach with a plug gap of .025in, but the Le Mans engine for the 100M had NA.10 plugs (see separate section). The firing order was 1, 3, 4, 2 and the ignition timing was 6° BTDC.

The control box was type RB106/1, mounted on the bulkhead behind the

engine. There was a separate fuse box, type SF6, with two fuses, of 50amp and 35amp capacity respectively. A solenoid starter switch type ST950 was fitted.

Headlamps were F700 with convex block-type lenses. Home market cars and cars for export markets driving on the left had headlamps dipping to the left, cars for European markets had double vertically dipping headlamps (in the case of France, with special yellow bulbs), and cars for overseas markets driving on the right had headlamps dipping to the right. The dip switch was foot operated, mounted to the left of the clutch pedal. On cars exported to certain American states but later on US export cars in general, it was necessary to fit sealed beam headlamps. US export cars therefore had special adaptors. Sometimes the sealed beam units may have been installed by American distributors, later on they were probably fitted at the factory.

Below the headlamps were sidelamps, type 488, incorporating flashing direction indicators. They had frosted white glass

lenses. The combined tail and stop lamps were also type 488, and also incorporated flashing direction indicators. Inevitably this meant that the brake lamps would flash. The flasher relay box was mounted on the left-hand inner wing behind the radiator. The flasher unit, type FL2 or FL3, was under the facia. Rear reflectors were not fitted originally but became a requirement in the home market in 1954. From approximately August 1954, small reflectors with chrome-plated rims were mounted on teardrop-shape pods above the rear lamps, on each side of the boot lid.

The numberplate lamp was type 467/2 with a single bulb and a chrome-plated housing. It was mounted behind the rear bumper. Two horns, type HF1748, were fitted, attached to the chassis crossmember in front of the radiator. They were finished in metallic tan. They were a matched pair of high-note and low-note horns. On the BN1, a windscreen wiper motor type CRT15 was used, but the BN2 model had a wiper motor type DR2 with a self-parking

The rear lamps are diminutive by modern standards (left). This BN2 model has the pod-mounted reflectors set into the panel above the lamps. The numberplate lamp is hidden within the rear bumper section.

A small detail, but this is the correct gasket for the headlamp with a tapered section. Note also the stainless steel beading between the wing and the shroud panel.

arrangement for the wipers. The wiper motor was mounted on the left-hand side under the scuttle. The wipers parked to the right on a RHD car, and to the left on a LHD car. The bezels where the wiper spindles came through the scuttle panel were painted on the BN1, chrome-plated on the BN2. The wiper arms were chrome-plated, with 9in long Trico Rainbow blades.

BODY AND BODY TRIM

The body was panelled partly in aluminium, partly in steel. In fact the early Warwick-built pre-production cars of 1952-53 (of which there were only 20) had all-aluminium bodies. The Longbridge-built production cars from May 1953 onwards with Jensen-built bodies always had their front shroud and rear tonneau panels in aluminium. These are the large panels which surround the bonnet and boot lid respectively. The wings and door panels were in steel. The front apron was in aluminium. Originally, the bonnet and boot lid were also in aluminium, but these were changed to steel panels early in production at body number 3397 for the bonnet, body number 4129 for the boot lid.

In structural terms, the external body panels were attached to a simple steel structure, created by the bulkhead and scuttle assembly, the front inner wings, the door pillars and door sills, a tonneau structure and the rear inner wings which formed the sides of the boot. The wings were bolted on. The front shroud was also bolted in place but the rear tonneau and lower body panel was rivetted to the luggage compartment frame. The bodyshell assembly was neatly divided in two major sub-assemblies, a front and a rear half.

The doors were supported on two hinges. The design of the hinges and door checkstraps was improved from body 5001, which also caused minor alterations to the hinge pillars, the front end assembly, the scuttle side assemblies and the doors

The sills and rear door pillars (right) are covered with these patterned aluminium plates. Note the outer door seal of black rubber on the pillar.

There is some variation possible in the door hinges and hinge pillars – this is the early type (left). It may also be noted that there is no stitching around the door pocket on this car. The Furflex trim strips forming the door seals are colour-coded to match the trim. The strengthening plate at the bottom of the pillar is not original.

The boot lid hinges (right) are a standard type. The retainers just in front of the hinges perform the same function for the hood and for the tonneau cover.

With the louvred bonnet and the strap, this is Peter Ellis's M-specification car which shows the bonnet prop in operation and also has the correct type of air trunking.

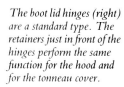

From this angle, the numberplate lamp can be seen (above). The rear numberplate is attached to a bracket mounted on the lower body panel. This is the correct position for the boot lid handle when the boot is closed. The style of escutcheon for the handle is the same for all Big Healeys.

The clean and uncluttered lines of the 100 (left) make this car truly 'a joy for ever'. Even the modest ornamentation seems to follow the basic design in a totally logical way.

themselves. There were no external door handles. At the top of the doors were two sockets for fitting the loose sidescreens, with chrome-plated surrounds. Patterned aluminium plates covered the door sills and the rear door shuts. The door lock strikers were chrome-plated; from body 2236 their design was changed, necessitating also changes to the shut pillars and their cover plates. The door seals were Furflex strips, colour-coded to the interior trim colour, with an additional black weatherstrip on the lock pillar at the rear of the door opening.

The bonnet was hinged at the front. The hinge plate at the front gave double thickness in this area, otherwise the bonnet was single skin, with a brace across the back, and two longitudinal braces forming an angle with its apex at the bonnet lock. The bonnet lock was centrally mounted on the scuttle, with a remote control under the facia. It incorporated a safety catch. There were three different types of bonnet lock. At body 1950, the catch was improved with a lock nut in place of a lock ring for the striker pin. At body 3801, the remote control mechanism was improved. The bonnet was propped open, the black-painted prop being fitted at the right-hand side of the engine compartment at the back. The closed bonnet rested on six rubber buffers, two at the back and two on each side.

The boot lid had external hinges, of chrome-plated Mazak. Apart from the additional hinge plate giving double thickness at the front, it was also single skin, fitted with two braces angled from the lock. The boot had an automatic boot stay fitted to the front left-hand corner of the boot lid. The boot lid was opened by a lockable handle at the bottom. The lock was operated by the same key as the ignition lock. The handle should be vertical when the boot lid is closed. The handle and its long, triangular escutcheon were chrome-plated. In the bottom right-hand corner of the boot lid was the name badge, cast in zinc

The combination of satin-finish radiator grille bars and a bright surround is correct. The style and position of the front badges can also be seen.

Good examples of the subtlety of body trim are the distinctive side flashes and the elegant swage line from the flash back to the rear wheel arch (below). The narrow air vent hidden by the flash can just be seen.

Two types of badge may be found on the boot lid. The early 1953-54 cars have this 'Austin of England' script, also found on Austin saloons of the period.

Later models have their own identity, with this 'Austin-Healey' script, which was carried forward also to the six cylinder models.

or brass and chrome-plated. Originally this was a script badge reading 'Austin of England' but in approximately August 1954 (the exact time is not known) it was changed to 'Austin-Healey'.

The body was wonderfully free of ornamentation. The radiator grille was of a very simple design, with a chrome-plated surround and vertical bars (43 of them, to be precise) which were brass, finished in a special satin-finish chrome plating. On the left-hand side of the radiator grille was lightning flash with the number '100' picked out in red. Originally the numbers were ¾in high, but during 1953 they were made 1in high. Above the grille was a chrome-plated winged badge with an 'Austin-Healey' script in red. On the side of each front wing was a chrome-plated flash, fitted over a small air vent (these were not very effective!). The flashes should always be fitted with the thinner, pointed end forward.

A simple swage line ran from the flash back along the wing and door, and to the

The beading behind the front apron is normally black, and it can be seen how the apron completely fills the gap between body and bumper (right). Note that the overriders do not have backing plates.

The bumper brackets are black, and at the back come through the lower body panel (right). This 1954 model has had reflectors fitted on the bumper. This picture also shows the rear lamp in detail.

The bumpers have a section with a single central groove (above). The overriders are a standard type of design. Note also the correct 45-degree angle to the end of the exhaust tailpipe.

rear wheel arch. On the BN1 model this swage line was not continued behind the rear wheel arch, but possibly at some stage during BN2 production the swage line was continued to the rear bumper. Expert opinion differs on when exactly the swage line was continued all the way back, and there is no change point recorded in the parts list.

A number of other changes were implemented on the BN2 model. The most important body change was that the front wheel arch was cut higher into the wing, 1¼in more when measured from the piping at the top where the wing joins the shroud. Because the forward continuation of the swage line would then hit the wheel arch below the top, the paint dividing line on BN2s painted in two-tone schemes was given a small hockey stick return where it ran into the wheelarch. However, the bottom colour of the car should go right up to the wheel arch itself.

The piping where the wings join the main body was actually a strip of stainless steel and was therefore a bright silver colour on all cars. Below the headlamps, however, was T-section Vynide piping which may be black or body colour. The piping behind the front apron below the radiator grille was probably always black. Front and rear bumpers were of similar design, with a section with a central groove. Both were fitted with overriders, to a standard Wilmot Breeden pattern of the period, with a central vertical groove. There was black plastic seating between bumpers and overriders. The front bumper did not have a hole for a starting handle. The bumper brackets were painted black; at the front they passed below the body, at the rear they passed through the lower rear body panel with rubber grommets. A front numberplate (backing plate) was usually fitted to home market cars, but was often deleted on export models. The rear numberplate was fitted to an adjustable bracket, screwed to the rear body panel.

The adjustable windscreen was a work of art and has rightly become one of the most

The intricate windscreen pillars allow for the lowering of the screen (below).

In the lowered position (above), the windscreen pillars fit into sockets mounted in the wing beading. The springs keep the windscreen tensioned. With the windscreen lowered (top), the car looks even more rakish.

famous features of the 100. With a curved windscreen – and with the general shape of the scuttle – it was not possible to incorporate a traditional fold-flat screen, still considered *de rigueur* on many sports cars. The solution was to mount the windscreen assembly on short, chrome-plated half pillars. By undoing a knurled nut either side, it was revealed that the actual windscreen was fitted on hinged links. The screen could then be lifted forward into a lower, more horizontal position. A pin in each bottom corner would locate the lowered screen, fitting into chrome-plated feet fixed in the joint between the wings and the shroud. Two springs were fitted to keep the lowered screen tensioned. The side pillars of the actual windscreen assembly were painted body colour, the glass being fitted in a chrome-plated frame. The glass was always laminated; early on it may have been supplied by Lancegaye, later by Triplex. A heavy black rubber apron provided a seal to the scuttle when the windscreen is in the upright position.

In the space between the radiator and the grille was a central vertical dividing panel, and on each side immediately in front of the radiator was an x-bracing. The left-hand one of these was supposedly slightly bent on 100M cars to allow easy installation of the special camshaft, without having to remove the engine. Similarly, on 100M cars the support strut for the front shroud on the left-hand side of the engine bay was slightly notched, to allow for the installation of the special cold air box found on these cars (see the 100M section which follows).

As has previously been mentioned, the completed chassis and body assembly was painted together by Jensens, so the main body colour should be found on all parts of the chassis and body, including the underside, inside the wings, in the engine bay and so on. The exception is that apparently some white cars had the front of the chassis from the door hinge pillars forward painted black. On two-tone cars, the lower body sides were painted in their different colour afterwards, the surrounding areas being masked off.

INTERIOR TRIM, BOOT AND HOOD

The two bucket seats had seat squabs which swung forward for access to the tonneau and the battery hatch. The cushions could be removed. The seat buckets were built up on wooden bases. Seats were upholstered in

The front footwells (left) are carpeted but the driver has this rubber heel mat with an 'Austin' script in the centre (just out of sight). The pedals and pedal rubbers seen here are correct, as is the accelerator.

An undoubtedly original interior (above) with a well-worn look after 35 years! The curious two-tone effect of the seat in this picture has been greatly exaggerated by flash lighting and is not apparent on the real seat. Not all seats have contrast piping but this light blue-grey is correct for blue seats. The floor covering under and behind the seats is Armacord.

leather, but with Vynide on non-wearing parts, including the backs of the squabs. Both squabs and cushions had a bolster edge surrounding central panels with five flutes. Sometimes the seat piping was in a contrast colour; for details, please refer to the list of colour schemes. Seat cushions were made from Dunlopillo foam rubber.

On the early cars, both seats could be adjusted only by taking out the setpins which held the base of the seat to the floor; the seat could then be adjusted to one of five positions, with holes for adjustment in the seat frame. However, from body number 1001, a slide was introduced for adjusting the driver's seat, while at the same time the passenger seat was made non-adjustable and was raised on additional 5/8in wooden packing strips. This change coincided with the deletion of the adjustable steering column.

There was carpet in front of the seats, over the gearbox tunnel and in the footwells. This was Karvel, laid over underfelt and held in place by press stud fasteners. On the driver's side was a black rubber heel mat with the word 'Austin' in script. The colour of the carpet matched the seats. Under and behind the seats the floorcovering was in Armacord mats. Originally these also matched the general interior trim colour, but replacements are now available only in black and blue.

The door trim casings were in plywood, and the interior trim panels were in plywood or millboard. All were covered in Vynide to match the seat colour. The doors incorporated generous glove or map pockets, again lined with Vynide. The early door casings were plain, later on they were finished with a row of stitching around the door pocket aperture, approximately 3/8in from the edge. Inside the door pocket was a pull cord to activate the door lock. There was also a chrome-plated door handle at the rear of the door at the top, easily reached from the outside. Along the tops of the doors, the facia rail and the edge of the rear tonneau were aluminium trim strips, all of which had the body number stamped on the back.

On later cars such as this BN2 (above), a row of stitching is found around the door pocket. Note the pull cord for releasing the door lock from the inside, and the two-piece lining for the door pocket.

The door tops (left) are fitted with these aluminium strips, also found along the rear edge of the cockpit and across the top of the facia. There is another Furflex strip at the rear of the door. The inner door handle is designed to be reached easily from the outside, even with the hood and sidescreens erected. The rear of the two sidescreen mounting sockets can be seen.

The hood simply stows away behind the seats (right), fighting for space with the spare wheel which pokes through from the boot in this Vynide bag. The floor of the tonneau and the battery hatch are also covered in Armacord.

The boot is lined with Armacord mats (above). This tool roll is a modern reproduction but in the correct oil cloth material and to the original pattern. Note the fuel filler cap, the strap holding the spare wheel in place and the battery master switch (just visible in the compartment to the left of the spare wheel).

On the propshaft tunnel between the seats was a centre armrest, with a fluted leather top and Vynide sides. It was detachable, mounted with Tenax fasteners, and there was carpet underneath. While the rear part of the propshaft tunnel was fixed, the front part could be removed, as could the entire gearbox cover. A small ashtray with a chrome-plated swivel top was set in the gearbox cover.

One of the perennial problems of the Healeys was the excessive heat which could build up in the footwells. Therefore, there was a separate fresh air intake under the facia on the right-hand side. This was operated by a butterfly valve with a control to the right of the heater. From the valve, a trunk of coated paper (which tends to sag badly) ran forward on the right-hand side of the engine compartment, to just in front of the radiator. From body number 5746, this trunking was extended further forward. At the same time, heat insulation of the left-hand footwell was improved, with extended asbestos shielding on the engine compartment side, better-quality underfelt and other modifications.

The heater itself has been described previously (see section on cooling system), but it is also worth mentioning that it had two pipes which fed hot air to demister outlets just below the windscreen. The two outlets were body coloured and each had two slots.

Under the facia on the passenger side was a parcel shelf, with a Vynide covered edge and carpet covering for the shelf itself.

Always on the left-hand side under the facia was the wiper motor, attached to a body colour bracket. The flasher unit for the direction indicators was also found here. On the BN1 model, the two overdrive relays were mounted under the facia on the driver's side. Of the major controls not previously described the accelerator pedal was of the organ type, with a pointed top end. It was mounted at an angle and had two grooves but no rubber covering.

The spare wheel protruded through from the boot to the tonneau area on the right-hand side and had a Vynide cover. The battery hatch was covered in Armacord, and was held in place when closed by two straps with Lift-the-Dot fasteners to the heelboard. In the boot itself, the petrol tank was covered by an Armacord mat colour-coded to match the interior; apparently, the fit was improved on the BN2 model by a seam following the rear edge of the petrol tank. The spare wheel shelf was covered in Armacord, and the spare wheel was held in place by a tie bar and a leather strap, fixed to a bracket below the shelf.

On the left-hand side of the boot was a cubby hole where the battery master switch was situated. This was also the normal home for the tool roll, which was made from black oil cloth. A full set of tools was supplied, and the spanners were marked 'Superslim'. Details will be found in the parts list. The wheel hammer was loose, but bags were provided for the jack and its handle. A starting handle was not supplied.

The hood was made from Vynide

The hood catches are fixed to brackets on the windscreen pillars (also used for the tension springs when the screen is lowered). This is by and large the correct pattern of hood, although it is a replacement made from a later type fabric.

covered canvas. It was blue on Healey Blue cars, and black on most others (see colour list). The hoodframe had two bows, with collapsible side members connecting to the front rail. The hoodframe was painted grey and was attached inside the car, on each side of the body behind the doors. The folded hood stowed away in the tonneau area. When raised it was fixed with Tenax fasteners to the rear tonneau panel and the rear wings, and was held down by two retainers in front of the boot lid hinges. There was also a turnbutton fastener just behind each door. All of these fittings performed the same functions for the tonneau cover. Finally, the raised hood was held tight by a strap on each side fixed to a press stud inside the rear quarters.

At the front, the hood fastened to the windscreen pillar by a chrome-plated over-centre catch on each side, latching on to small buttons at the top of the pillars. These buttons were also used for fastening the tension springs when the windscreen was lowered. There were three small rubber mushrooms on brackets on the hood front rail to act as buffers where the front rail touched the windscreen frame. The hood cover had a generously-sized one-piece clear plastic rear window.

The full-length tonneau cover with a centre zip was supplied as standard. Apart from using the hood fixings at the back, the tonneau cover was attached to three Tenax fasteners at the front, one to each side of the scuttle, and one by the mirror in the centre; the centre fastener always held the

The rear window seen here (above) is not quite the correct shape, being possibly a little too rounded at the ends. This car (in Spruce Green with Green trim) might originally have had a green hood.

The hood frame folds up like this (left), although it might be an idea to pull the hood cover clear at the back first! The frame is painted the correct light grey, as are the brackets where it is attached to the sides of the body behind the doors.

This rear window has a better shape, and the hood fabric is the correct type with a plain rather than patterned under-surface (never mind the water stains!).

Of the three different types of sidescreen, this is the final one with the full-length signalling flap (left). This is also the original type of sidescreen storage bag.

The later type of tonneau cover (above) with a supposedly better fit may still allow water to run down the inside of the door! The turnbuckle fastener at the back of the door should be on a little extra tab of its own. The tonneau cover would normally be the same colour as the hood – both in fact should be green on this Spruce Green car with Green trim.

passenger side of the tonneau cover in place. The original tonneau cover was widened and fitted with improved fasteners from body number 4606. The material and colour of the tonneau cover matched the hood.

Three different types of sidescreens were found as standard equipment. The first type was of rigid perspex with a chrome-plated frame to the bottom and to the front. From body number 1100, they were replaced by more conventional sidescreens with fabric-covered metal frames, incorporating a signalling flap in their lower half, and with chrome-plated beading round the edge. The original type of signalling flap was rectangular, with a small fabric triangle at the front. From body number 7258 the third type of sidescreen was introduced, with a deeper, full-length signalling flap, and chrome-plated beading to the front and top half of the sidescreen, as well as above the signalling flap. All sidescreens were located with pegs in two sockets on the

Note that the zip in the tonneau cover is off-set to the passenger side (above), giving the driver a little bit more elbow room when only the passenger seat is covered.

doors. Sidescreens with signalling flaps have a strap fixing to a press stud fastener on the door trim to keep the flap closed. An envelope for storing the sidescreens and tonneau cover was supplied.

DASHBOARD AND INSTRUMENTS

The facia panel was made of painted metal. It was usually dark blue on cars in Healey Blue, and mostly black on others. Normally the instrument panel was painted silver (except, it would seem, on John Wheatley's car photographed for this book!). Originally, the facia panel and instrument panel were separate pieces, but from body number 1855 they were made in one piece. Another change concerned the size of the slot for the steering column. When the adjustable steering column was discontinued the slot was reduced in width (at body 1001) from 2¼in to 1¾in.

The instrument panel was oval in shape and was set in front of the driver. The lay-

Both of the 100s illustrated on this page have the correct steering wheel, and neither has the adjustable steering column only found on the early cars. The instrument panel on John Wheatley's car is, unusually, the same dark blue colour as the main facia panel.

While this BN2 has the instrument panel in silver, it might have been more correct if the main panel had been black rather than the body colour. Comparing this with the previous photograph, it will be seen that the main difference is the transposition of the ignition lock and the overdrive switch, and the latter now has a round – as opposed to an hourglass-shaped – escutcheon.

out was always the same on left-hand drive and right-hand drive cars. The two larger instruments had dials finished with silver centres and black, dished peripheries; the smaller instruments had flat black dials. Figures and lettering were white (black in the centres of the two large instruments), and pointers were white but had black centre ends on the speedometer and rev counter. These two instruments also had quite a distinctive typeface for the numbers, whereas the typeface on the smaller instruments was plain.

From left to right, controls and instruments were found in the following order. First came a combined oil pressure and water temperature gauge: the oil pressure gauge in the upper half read to 100lb/sq in, and the water temperature gauge below read to 230° Fahrenheit (a Centigrade instrument was not available). Next followed a starter push-button set in a round bezel, and below it was the wiper switch in a hexagonal bezel. Then came the speedometer; the normal instrument read to 120mph (with a kilometres version available for export, reading to 200kph) in 20mph intervals. The speedometer incorporated mileage recorders for trip and total mileage. The trip meter was above and read to three figures plus decimal, the total mileage recorder below with five figures. The trip recorder had a re-set button behind and below the facia. To the left of this was the panel light switch. The speedometer also incorporated a red warning light for high beam. A 140mph speedometer as fitted to the 100S was found on some cars, if fitted with the Le Mans engine conversion and the alternative 3.66 rear axle ratio.

In the centre of the panel, immediately above the steering column, was a green warning lamp for the flashing indicators, in

a round chrome-plated bezel. On the other side of the column was the rev counter or tachometer, which read to 6000rpm in 1000rpm intervals, with a red line at 4800rpm. In the bottom of the rev counter was a red ignition warning lamp. To the right of the rev counter was the light switch in a hexagonal bezel. It was marked 'Side' and 'Head'; it was pulled to turn on the side and rear lamps, and then twisted to turn on the headlamps. Below, also in a hexagonal bezel, was the ignition lock, with a key number originally in the FA range but on later cars sometimes in the FP range. The same key operated the boot lid lock. Finally came the fuel gauge which was marked in quarter intervals. The four instruments were all set in chrome-plated bezels.

Immediately to the left of the instrument panel (or, on a left-hand drive car, to the right) was the flick switch for the overdrive, with an hour-glass shaped chrome-plated escutcheon, marked 'Overdrive' above and 'Normal' below the switch. The only

modification introduced on the BN2 model in 1955 was that the ignition lock and overdrive switch were transposed, and the overdrive switch was given a new round escutcheon.

In front of the passenger, towards the outside of the car, was a chrome-plated grab handle, set directly on the surface of the facia panel. Major controls not found on the facia included the heater blower rheostat switch positioned on the heater itself; the control for the separate fresh-air intake found on the right of the heater; and the choke control, found on the left of the heater. The bonnet release was under the facia, above the heater.

Above the facia, on the rear edge of the scuttle, was an aluminium trim strip matching the other trim strips to the door tops and rear cockpit edge. On the scuttle was a centrally-mounted Eversure rear view mirror, with a chrome-plated back and stem, incorporating a ball fitting for adjustment.

The 100M Model

Although not a factory-built 100M, Peter Ellis's BN1 has been fitted with the Le Mans engine modification kit and its under-bonnet appearance is authentic. Compared to engine pictures found previously in this book, it has the correct straight-type plug caps and the correct wire clips for the hose pipe. This picture also shows the steel dust grey engine very clearly, although the rocker cover and the oil filler cap are non-standard items.

This is the plate you would expect to find on a car with the Le Mans engine kit (below). The experts felt that this might be a reproduction cold-air box – the originals had rather crude welding seams along the edges!

Before the 100M model is discussed, it must be explained that in 1954 the Austin and Healey companies between them developed what was called the 'Le Mans' Engine Modification Kit. This kit was based on the engine modifications found on the works racing cars which ran in the 1953 Le Mans 24 hour race – hence the name. The 'Le Mans' engine kit was available from Austin, or Healey, under part number P.280. It could be retro-fitted to existing cars, or could be fitted to new cars by Healey, or by other dealers.

The 'Le Mans' kit consisted of the following parts: a pair of 1¾in carburettors, with special manifolds and four-stud fixing; a joint carburettor cold air box, on which was sometimes fitted a small plate proclaiming that 'This car has been fitted with a 'Le Mans' modification kit'; stronger valve springs; a high-lift camshaft; a steel face cylinder head gasket; and a distributor with a special advance curve (ignition timing set at 9° BTDC). NA.10 plugs were fitted. Apart from several other fittings, the kit also included a new left-hand support for the bonnet frame with a notch to clear the cold air box. With standard pistons and unchanged compression ratio, power output should improve to 100bhp at

4500rpm. If, in addition, the 8.1:1 high compression pistons were fitted, power output should be 110bhp at 4500rpm.

The kit could be installed with the engine in situ, but some dexterity was called for to extract the camshaft from the front (after the radiator was removed). In consequence the left-hand x-brace in front of the radiator was often bent slightly to one side to give sufficient clearance for replacing the camshaft.

With the introduction of the BN2 model, it was decided to offer cars with Le Mans engines ex-factory – the resulting model became the 100M. It was officially launched

The other characteristic of the 100M specification is this louvred bonnet (also seen on the green BN2 featured in this book). The strap should be more precisely centred between the louvres.

at the London Motor Show in October 1955, but it appears that some such cars had already been delivered to the USA before then. The 100M cars were fitted with the high compression pistons as well as the Le Mans kit. They also had a stiffer anti-roll bar, and were fitted with a louvred bonnet with leather strap. This bonnet had two rows of louvres, each with six louvres behind the strap and 14 in front. The rows of louvres were set towards each side of the bonnet, and as they follow the general shape of the bonnet they form a slight V-shape towards the front. Most 100M cars were finished in two-tone colour schemes, but around 30 per cent were finished in single colours. The two-tone colour schemes were also available on the standard model.

Apparently these cars were built at Longbridge with standard specification engines, but with the louvred bonnets already installed (by Jensen). As the cars came off the line, they were sent to Healeys at Warwick, where the Le Mans engine modification kit was installed. The cars were then sent back to Longbridge for despatch, mostly to export markets, particularly the USA.

Geoffrey Healey, Donald's son who played a very important part in the family firm in the fifties, has given a figure of 1159 cars for 100M production. John Wheatley, carrying out research in the microfilmed BN2 Longbridge build records, has come up with a figure of only 640 cars which can be identified by having a note scribbled on the build card to the effect that they had the louvred bonnet fitted. It must therefore be presumed that these 640 cars were the factory-built 100M cars, and the balance of 519 cars were other 100 models which were modified with the Le Mans kit at Warwick. The factory-built 100M only existed as a BN2, but all the parts required for modification could equally easily be fitted to a BN1.

We therefore have at least two categories of 100M cars: those that were designated as such at Longbridge, and can be called the factory-built cars; and those that were modified at Warwick after they had been delivered to the original owners. Also, as all the relevant parts could at the time be supplied to third parties, whether Austin dealers or private owners, there are cars which were modified to 100M specification without involving either Longbridge or Warwick. These modifications could have been done at the time, or well after production of the model had ceased. Confused? You will be.

Getting back on firmer ground, John Wheatley's research has also resulted in statistics according to which 544 of the 640 factory-built cars were for the USA (85 per cent), with only eight remaining in the UK. Of the rest, 58 went to various European destinations, 25 went overseas, and the last five were supplied in the UK for Personal Export Delivery. A total of 195 cars were in single colours, and 445 in two-tone schemes. White over Black was most popular (117 cars), but was outnumbered by the two different combinations of Red and Black if counted together (92 cars Red over Black, 71 cars Black over Red). The most popular single colour was White (62 cars). Green was least popular (five cars Spruce Green, three cars Florida Green). Two cars were finished in special two-tone schemes: one was White over Red, the other (which 'graced' the 1955 Motor Show stand) was Black over Pink!

Some 100M cars sport a radiator grille badge with an added letter M. It is questionable whether these were original, but some experts feel that such badges were fitted at Warwick to cars converted for specially favoured customers!

The 100S Model

Looming out of the mist and highly desirable, Frank Sytner's 100S (AHS/3905) originally went to Australia and has been re-imported in recent years – hence the give-away 'age-related' registration mark. The grille shape is noticeably different. This car has lost its grille-mounted 100S badge.

The special Lucas Le Mans type headlamps were found only on the 100S.

This was a very special car, built primarily with racing in mind. These cars were assembled by Healey at Warwick, although Jensen still provided the chassis and body assemblies, and the engines and gearboxes were supplied from the Morris Engines factory at Coventry (which had by now taken over the manufacture of the Austin-Healey engine from Longbridge).

The engine was fitted with an aluminium cylinder head developed by Weslake. This had the manifolds and carburettors on the right-hand side, so the plugs and other electrical equipment were moved to the left-hand side. The crankshaft was nitride hardened and various other modifications were made. The carburettors were SU H.6 1¾in; they had vertical bellhousings and a joint cold air box. High compression (8.3:1) pistons were fitted. The engine developed 132bhp at 4700rpm, and maximum torque was 168lb ft at 2500rpm. The engine was painted non-metallic dark green. The lubrication system included a combined oil filter and cooler, fitted on the upper of the two chassis crossmembers in front of the radiator. There was a twin-pipe exhaust system.

While the four-speed gearbox was essentially of the same BMC design as used in the BN2 model, it had a special close-

The dual exhaust pipe (left) coming out under the right-hand door was unique to the 100S but should probably be cut off at a 45-degree angle. Looking under the bonnet of a 100S (below), the bigger carburettors with vertical bellhousings mounted on the right of the head are a recognition point.

The unique White over Blue colour scheme was found on most 100S cars. The colour split is slightly different to that found on a BN2 or 100M in that the dividing line continues straight to the top of the front wheel arch. The perspex screen on this car is a little too low, by a matter of 1½in or so. The mirror is not original. The car should have an interior mirror, of the dipping type made by Lucas.

ratio gear cluster. Gearbox ratios were: first, 3.08; second, 1.91; third, 1.33; and direct top. An overdrive was not fitted. The spiral bevel type of rear axle was used; the standard final drive ratio was 2.92 to 1, but alternative ratios of 2.69, 3.66 and 4.125 were available.

The most important modification to the chassis was that Dunlop disc brakes were fitted to all four wheels. Stiffer shock absorbers were used. The steering wheel was adjustable, and had a laminated wood rim and aluminium spokes. Tyres were Dunlop 5.50-15 racing tyres.

The electrical system incorporated a high-output dynamo, Lucas C39PV2, and special Le Mans type headlamps. A single 12 volt battery was fitted in the passenger footwell, with a 38 AH capacity. The battery master switch was relocated under the bonnet. The sparking plugs were Champion NA.10.

All the external body panels were in aluminium. The radiator grille was smaller and more oval in shape. An elongated S was added to the grille badge. Bumpers were not fitted, and there was no provision for a hood or sidescreens. A low one-piece Perspex windscreen was fitted, and there were no windscreen wipers. The bonnet was louvred, and was held in place by a

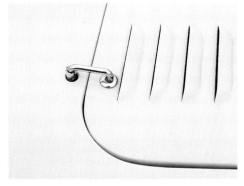

Also unique to the 100S are these two clips holding the rear of the bonnet in place (right).

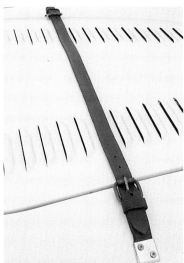

The louvred bonnet with its strap (left) was similar to that of the 100M, but was made from aluminium, whereas most 100M cars had steel bonnets.

At first glance the interior is similar to the standard model. There are numerous detail differences, most obviously the seats with plain rather than fluted centre panels, and backrests incorporating three vertical ventilation slots.

Another distincitive feature of the 100S is the quick-release fuel filler cap on the rear tonneau panel (below).

The aluminium spoke steering wheel with a wood rim (right) is correct on the 100S but some cars have single long slots in the spokes. Instead of the overdrive switch an oil thermometer is fitted. The single 12 volt battery lives in the passenger footwell. This car has its gearlever off-set to the left but some 100S cars seem to have a more central gearlever which may suggest an alternative gearbox design.

There is not a lot of boot space left when a 20 gallon tank is fitted (right). The spare wheel has been moved over to the left, unlike the standard 100.

leather strap, and by two small hooks (Dzus fasteners) at the rear of the bonnet. Most cars were painted White over Lobelia Blue, a specially formulated paint supplied by Dockers. These colours were chosen because white and blue were the official US racing colours. The colour split followed the swage line pressed in the body, forward of this to the top of the front wheel arch, while the colour split line behind the rear wheel arch weas slightly different to the colour split on a two-tone BN2. The wheels were painted white.

The boot was largely filled by a 20 gallon petrol tank. The filler neck came through the rear tonneau panel just behind the cockpit, and a quick-release aluminium filler cap was fitted. Two electric fuel pumps were fitted. The spare wheel was relocated to the left-hand side.

Interior trim was rather spartan. The standard trim colour was blue with white piping. The seat backrests each incorporated three vertical slots to keep the driver cool. The facia was like that of the ordinary 100, but an oil temperature gauge was fitted where you would normally expect to find the overdrive switch. The speedometer read to 140mph; a heater was not fitted. The equipment included a special quick-lift jack, with dual front and rear jacking points.

The 100S was developed during 1953 and 1954. The 'S' was actually supposed to stand for Sebring, where a development car had come first in class in 1954, as well as third overall. The production model 100S made its competition debut in the 1955 Sebring race. There were five works development or special test cars, which carried SPL prefixed chassis numbers. The 50 production cars were delivered from February to November 1955. These had chassis numbers prefixed AHS, and five batches of chassis numbers were issued, as follows: AHS/3501 to 3510; AHS/3601 to 3610; AHS/3701 to 3710; AHS/3801 to 3810; and AHS/3901 to 3910. There was a single batch of engine numbers, from 1B/222701 to 1B/222750. Some engine numbers were suffixed with the letter C. Body numbers ran from 31 to 81; the odd number out which was not used on a production car was 33.

Of the 50 production cars, only six were originally delivered in the UK. The USA took 25, and two went to Canada. Five went to Australia and two to New Zealand. Two each went to France and Sweden. The last six cars went singly to a variety of destinations of which Madagascar was possibly the most unlikely! It is thought that of the 55 cars built, at least 37 are still in existence.

The original chassis number plate (which makes no mention of Austin!) and the body number plate above it are both found on the bulkhead behind the engine.

The facia panel is covered in Vynide and carries this small plate which clearly says all there is to say.

Production Changes

Changes by chassis (car) number

138031 May 53
First Longbridge-built car.

140205 Aug 53
New type overdrive, reduction ratio changed from 32.4 per cent to 28.6 per cent. Propshaft shortened. Gearbox mainshaft lengthened.

146476 Oct 53
Rear axle bumper brackets modified to improve clearance to tyres.

148528 Nov 53
Accelerator control rod shortened.

148921 (LHD) Nov 53
148987 (RHD) Dec 53
Rear springs changed from ¼in negative camber to ½in positive camber, for improved ground clearance.

148935 Dec 53
Front hub dust cap extractor added to tool kit.

148937 Dec 53
Carburettor jet needles changed from AH2 to QW (tapered) for better fuel economy.

149628 (LHD) Dec 53
149648 (RHD)
Improved flexible section to exhaust pipe.

149903 (LHD) Dec 53
149950 (RHD)
Modified handbrake lever for better clearance to propshaft tunnel.

149930 (LHD) Dec 53
149950 (RHD)
Adjustable steering column replaced by fixed. Adjustable driver's seat with slides introduced (body number 1001).

149983 (LHD) Dec 53
Modified oil pressure gauge pipe and securing clip on LHD cars only.

151608 Jan 54
Modified petrol tank straps.

152233 (LHD) Feb 54
152420 (RHD)
Stronger eight-leaf rear springs fitted intermittently, on all cars from 154647, Apr 1954. Also body modifications necessary for spring clearance.

153855 (LHD) Mar 54
153857 (RHD)
Stiffer front shock absorbers.

155284 May 54
Bolts with D-shaped heads to coupling flange between overdrive and propshaft.

156814 May 54
Brake pipe union threads changed from ANF to UNF.

156840 May 54
Battery fixing rods, threads changed from BSF to UNF.

157302 May 54
Modified bush with oil hole for third speed mainshaft in gearbox.

157624 Jun 54
Steering cross and side tubes with non-adjustable ball pins instead of adjustable ones.

159257 Jul 54
Hide-faced hammer in tool kit replaced by lead-faced hammer.

159802 Aug 54
Stronger road wheels with modified hub section.

160315 Aug 54
Rubber cover to petrol pump introduced.

161885
Last car with pre-unified car and engine numbers.

219001 Sep 54
First car with unified car/engine number.

219137 (LHD) Sep 54
219258 (RHD)
Steering gear: screw-type rocker shaft adjustment instead of selective shim adjustment.

219137 Sep 54
Co-axial front shock absorbers with larger valve chambers.

220088 Oct 54
Co-axial rear shock absorbers with larger valve chambers.

221012 Oct 54
Improved rubber mountings for gearbox and overdrive, packing piece deleted, threads changed from BSF to UNF.

221404 Nov 54
Front suspension and fulcrum pins, threads changed from BSF to UNF. Front brake cylinders reduced from 1in to ⅞in for improved brake balance.

221536 Nov 54
Hypoid rear axle introduced. Wider rear brakes. Shorter propshaft. Rear axle threads changed from BSF to UNF. Stiffer rear springs (changed at approx body no. 6478). Various attendant changes to rear axle assembly.

222571 Dec 54
Rear hubs, threads changed from BSF to UNF.

222781 Dec 54
Brake pedal lever strengthened.

223136 Jan 55
Modified front brake pipes, minor changes to front suspension and steering box bracket.

223155 Jan 55
Dynamo with longer rear bearing cover.

223220 Jan 55
Rear spring shackle pins, threads changed from BSF to UNF.

223384 Jan 55
Accelerator control rod, threads changed from BSF to UNF.

225780 May 55
Oil-filled ignition coil introduced.

227339 Jul 55
New type of jack.

227524 Jul 55
Modified front brake hose brackets.

227560 Jul 55
Rear flexible brake hoses encased in spring steel armour to prevent chafing.

228012 Aug 55
Rear axle oil filler plug moved from gear carrier to rear of axle casing. Rear hub lock nut threads now handed – left- and right-hand threads instead of both having right-hand threads.

228047 Aug 55
BN2 model introduced. Four-speed gearbox, new clutch, separate casting for clutch housing. Overdrive now on third and fourth gears. One instead of two overdrive relays, and simplified wiring. Wider front brake drums, taper roller bearings to front hubs. Revised front spring rates. Self-parking wipers. Ignition lock and overdrive switch transposed on facia.

228487 Sep 55
Modified gearlever.

228932 Sep 55
Steering tubes and levers of alternative design.

229080 Oct 55
New type of jack.

229207 Oct 55
Reverse check plunger to change speed cross shaft modified for easier engagement of reverse gear.

229654 Nov 55
Lead hammer in tool kit replaced by copper hammer.

229626 (LHD) Dec 55
230078 (RHD)
Front suspension grease nipples, threads changed from BSF to UNF.

230361 Jan 56
Distributor with pre-tilted contact breakers introduced. Lucas part number changed from 40320 to 40495 (Austin part no. from 3H2313 to 11B479).

230490 Jan 56
Shims deleted from overdrive mainshaft bearing plate and spring plate. New adaptor plate gearbox to overdrive.

230660 (RHD) Feb 56
230684 (LHD)
Longer bolts to front coil spring seats.

230978 (RHD) Mar 56
231109 (LHD)
Cam Gears steering box and idler, with increased diameter of rocker shaft, fitted instead of Burman steering gear.

233455 Jul 56
Last car.

Changes by engine number

139116 Oct 53
Distance collar added between carburettors and adaptors.

139916 Nov 53
Longer carburettor support brackets and adaptor studs.

207106 Apr 54
Self-locking nuts replace nuts with split pins to main bearing caps.

207112 Apr 54
New type of Tecalemit oil filter (Purolator filter not changed).

213325 May 54
Modified adaptor to oil filter: filter now vertical rather than angled, for improved clearance to engine mounting.

213399 Jun 54
Self-locking bolts to con rods.

214145 Jul 54
Flywheel with longer locating dowels for clutch.

224820 Mar 55
Piston top rings with chrome-plated periphery.

225030 Apr 55
Valve rocker brackets commonalized with Taxi Diesel engine.

225568 May 55
Thermostat with jiggle pin to prevent blockage of vent hole.

226095 Jun 55
Crankcase rear cover dowelled to crankcase to prevent oil leaks. Engine rear plate screwed to rear main bearing cap.

228079 Aug 55
Longer setscrews for oil filter adaptor.

231968 Apr 56
Gearlever shortened by 2in.

At some point in 1955, the con rod bolts were shortened and were fitted with thinner washers for improved clearance to crankcase (possibly from engine number 222899).

Other mechanical changes

From gearbox number 5146 (in Mar 1954?), a modified third speed mainshaft with larger and stronger gear teeth was fitted. First speed mainshaft and laygear were modified to suit. Take care to use correctly matched sets of gears when rebuilding gearboxes.

From overdrive number 28/1292/3773, in 1954, the closed type bracket for the overdrive solenoid was replaced by an open bracket with a stoneguard, and a rubber cover was fitted to the overdrive switch.

From overdrive number 28/1292/9493 (and on the optional close-ratio overdrive from number 22/1312/37), the overdrive planet carrier was made of solid construction, and the front and middle thrust washers were deleted.

Changes by body number

Figures in parentheses indicate approximate chassis number. Please note that the chassis number change points are approximate as body numbers were never issued in strict order by chassis numbers (or, arguably, vice versa).

21 (138931) May 53
First body fitted to a Longbridge-built car.

1001 (149930) Dec 53
Adjustable steering column discontinued. Steering column slot in facia reduced in size. Driver's seat adjustable on slides. Packing strips fitted to raise passenger seat.

1100 (149952) Dec 53
Rigid one-piece sidescreen replaced by two-piece sidescreen with signalling flap.

1855 (151795) Feb 54
Facia and instrument panel now in one piece.

1950 (152100) Feb 54
Improved bonnet catch, lock nut replaces lock ring for striker pin.

1953 (152233) Feb 54
Floor panel, front and rear end assemblies, and casings for rear quarter and wheelarch all changed to allow for new rear springs.

2236 (152600) Mar 54
Door lock strikers fitted with tapped plate and packing plate. Attendant changes to shut pillars and cover plates.

3052 Apr 54
Battery access panel hinges fitted with screws instead of being spot-welded.

3245 (155512) May 54
Raised dome on gearbox cover for overdrive switch, to prevent the risk of short-circuiting.

3397 (156120) May 54
Bonnet changed from aluminium to steel.

3800 Jun 54
Bonnet remote control bracket separated from bracket for facia and driving mirror.

3801 Jun 54
Bonnet lock remote control improved.

4129 (158100) Jun 54
Boot lid changed from aluminium to steel.

4606 (159339) Jul 54
Wider tonneau cover with improved fasteners.

Not known Aug 54
Boot lid badge changed from 'Austin of England' to 'Austin-Healey'. Rear reflectors fitted.

5001 (219046) Sep 54
Improved door hinges and check straps. Attendant changes to front end assembly, hinge pillars, scuttle side assemblies and doors.

5639 Sep 54
Improved boot floor mat.

5746 (219622) Oct 54
Heat insulation to left-hand footwell improved. Asbestos shielding extended, improved heat deflector to gearbox, and fresh-air intake hose brought forward to radiator grille.

7258 (222600) Jan 55
Third type of sidescreen with full-length signalling flap.

10031 (228047) Aug 55
First BN2 body. Front wing with 1¼in higher wheel cut-out. Ignition lock and overdrive switch transposed on facia. Modified gearbox cover and tunnel. Possibly introduced at this time (possibly later), rear wing with swage line continued behind wheelarch.

10067 Aug 55
Modified door casings.

11143 (229180) Nov 55
Improved rubber seal between door and scuttle to prevent water entering at this point.

14634 Jul 56
Last body number issued.

There are a number of other, smaller changes found in the parts lists, or sometimes quoted in the Austin Service Journal, which cannot be tied down to a specific change point in car/chassis, engine or body numbers, nor to a specific date. However, most such changes probably concern parts where the old and the new part were interchangeable.

OPTIONS, EXTRAS AND ACCESSORIES

Not very many factory-fitted options or extras were available. All cars were supplied complete with wire wheels, overdrive, a tonneau cover, sidescreens and, in most cases, a heater.

An alternative rear axle ratio of 9/33 (3.667:1) was quoted for the early spiral bevel axle. Similarly, a close-ratio overdrive with a 22 per cent reduction was available. Intended for the competition-minded owner were the Alfin brake drums, available in two types for cars with narrow brake drums. The harder front shock absorbers, standard from chassis 153855 on, could be fitted to earlier cars if desired, and the stiffer rear springs, standard from chassis 152233 on, could also be retro-fitted to earlier cars. A stiffer anti-roll bar was available.

Available under Austin part numbers (but probably never fitted to cars on the assembly line) were a racing-type silencer, waterproof plug caps, aero screen assemblies, and petrol tanks of either 15 or 25 gallons, with special straps. A 140mph speedometer seems to have been fitted to a few cars; probably this was the instrument found on the 100S model. Intriguingly, one brochure suggests that not only could 6.00-15 tyres be fitted as an alternative, but 6.00-16 tyres could be fitted, in Road Speed or racing pattern. Yet nowhere can I find any mention of 16in wheels!

A few cars were fitted with chrome-plated wire wheels, although this was not a regular option. Some cars may have been fitted with whitewall tyres. Some cars may have been fitted with radios on the assembly line. Two-tone paint finish became a factory option on the BN2 model from late 1955 onwards (see colour section for details).

The Le Mans engine conversion kit, with or without high compression pistons, was available for retro-fitting to standard cars, apart from being fitted to the 100M models. Similarly, the louvred bonnet was available to modify non-M cars – cost, from Healeys at Warwick, a mere £15 10s! The demarcation line between standard cars and 'genuine' 100M cars begins to blur . . .

The Healey company at Warwick also made many other items of additional equipment available. According to a 1956-dated price list the following items were offered (in addition to those mentioned):

8.1:1 high compression pistons (for standard or Le Mans engines)
Fitted luggage
Chromium-plated exhaust tail-pipe trim
Chromium-plated headlamp stone guards
Chromium-plated stone guards for pass and fog lamps
Chromium-plated badge bar
Chromium-plated luggage rack
Chromium-plated rocker cover and air cleaners (on exchange basis)
Leather covering for facia panel, to match trim colour
Leather covering for cockpit mouldings, to match trim colour
Leather bonnet strap
Wing mirror(s)
Two-tone colour finish (presumably as partial repainting of existing cars)
Wood-rim steering wheel (non adjustable type)
Fibreglass hard top, normal or wrap-around rear window (supplied with sliding side windows)
Child's occasional seat, to match trim (this fitted over the propshaft tunnel, between the two seats)
Plain perspex sidescreens
Motorola radio
Cigar lighter
Electric clock
Ammeter
Oil temperature gauge
Fog lamp (Lucas SFT.576 or SFT.700)
Spot lamp (Lucas SLR.576 or SLR.700)
Reversing lamp

It is also probable that there was a variety of contemporary after-market accessories available from other sources, notably in the USA. For instance, several different types of rocker covers, some of polished cast aluminium, others ribbed, are known.

IDENTIFICATION, DATING AND PRODUCTION FIGURES

The chassis (or car) numbers allocated to the Austin-Healey 100 were issued in a series which was shared with other Austin products using the same basic engine design. This series of numbers had begun with 1 back in 1945 for the first Austin Sixteen (type BS1), and other models sharing these numbers were the A70 (Hampshire and Hereford models, as well as the Countryman and Pick-up varieties),

the A90 Atlantic, and the FX3 Taxicab and FL1 Hire Car.

There appear to be several first chassis numbers for the first Austin-Healey 100. In fact, the very first cars built at Warwick had prototype style chassis numbers which were prefixed SPL. However, the first proper chassis number allocated to a Warwick-built car was 133234. This number was prefixed BN1. The prefix indicated that this was a B-class (2000-3000cc engine size) car, with N for open two-seater body and 1 for first series. On cars with left-hand drive the BN1 prefix was followed by an L. The first Longbridge-built car had chassis number BN1-L/138031, and right-hand drive cars followed from chassis number BN1/138975. Most 1953-54 Austin-Healey chassis numbers were issued in batches of 100 numbers out of the main series of numbers.

Some of the very early prototype and pre-production cars had engine numbers which were lower than the normal series of engine numbers. The parts list quotes the first engine number as 136894; this engine was in fact fitted to car number BN1-L/138031. The engine numbers, like the chassis numbers, were taken out of the main series of engine numbers shared with the related models. Engine numbers were prefixed 1B (which should be read *one* B) and sometimes engine numbers were suffixed with the letter M. A suffix letter M does *not* indicate that it is an 'M' specification engine. The letter M was used also on other Austin engines – even on the Austin Sevens of the 1920s and 1930s – and I believe that the M may stand for 'Motor'. It was used merely to indicate that this was an engine number, rather than a chassis number, in those cases where there might be some doubt as to which number was which. However, it has also been suggested that the M suffix stands for Morris, and was found only on the later engines made by the Morris Engines Branch at Coventry.

Once proper production had got under way, the following batches of engine numbers were allocated to the Austin-Healey engines, as opposed to the A70 or Taxi engines.

139001 to 140000
205001 to 206000
206501 to 207481
213001 to 215092

In August 1954, there was a major change to the chassis and engine number system. From then on, Austin cars had the *same* number for the chassis and for the engine. I believe that the way this was achieved was by numbering the engines first, and when an engine was installed in a car, the engine number was then transcribed as the chassis/car number. Austin called this system 'the unified car/engine number system' and from then on we find the expression 'car/engine number', sometimes abbreviated to 'c/e no.'.

Officially, the last Austin-Healey 100 built before the unified car/engine number system was introduced was chassis number 161023 (on 31 August 1954), but in the following weeks another 20 cars were built with old-style numbers, possibly to use up engines held in stock which had old numbers. The highest chassis number issued to a pre-unified car was therefore 161885.

Since by August 1954 the engine number series had jumped far ahead of the chassis number series, it was necessary to re-start the chassis number series at 219000. In fact, 219000 was an A70 saloon, and the first Austin-Healey 100 with a unified car/engine number was 219001. Obviously this also had engine number 219001. Otherwise, the system continued much as before, with batches of numbers being allocated to Austin-Healeys. After the A70 models were discontinued, only the Taxicab and Hire Car types shared the number series.

In August 1955, the BN2 model was introduced, with the four-speed gearbox and other changes as detailed elsewhere. The last BN1 model was car/engine number 228026. There was then a gap before the BN2 model began, with car/engine number 228047. The prefix for the car/chassis number was altered to BN2 or BN2-L. The engine number prefix was still 1B. There was actually a small overlap, because of the practice of allocating engine numbers as chassis numbers to the cars as they were built. The parts list quotes seven numbers lower than 228047 as having been allocated to cars with BN2 specification. In fact my researches suggest that there may have been as many as 15 such cars, ranging from car/engine number 227489 (if not lower) to car/engine number 228026. (If 228026 was in fact a BN2 specification car, the last BN1 would be 228025.) The BN2 went into production on 19 August 1955.

Once the change-over had been sorted out, the car/engine number series

Early 1953-54 BN1 models have this plate giving car and engine numbers on the scuttle side casing just in front of the door. This type of white plastic plate is common also to Austin saloons of the period.

In addition, these early 1953-54 BN1s also have a chassis number plate on the right-hand chassis rail by the master cylinder bracket. Later BN1s and BN2s with unified car/engine numbers had a single 'car/engine number' plate on the bulkhead behind the engine (see picture of a 100-Six plate later in the book).

continued until the last Austin-Healey 100, which had car number BN2-L/233455 and engine number 1B/233455, built on 16 July 1956.

Dating an Austin-Healey 100 by the car/chassis number is a little difficult, bearing in mind that after the introduction of the unified car/engine number system chassis numbers were not issued in strict order. Therefore the following table must be regarded as an approximation only, as far as the 1954/55 and 1955/56 changeover points are concerned:

1953: from chassis number 133234 to chassis number 150363
1954: from chassis number 150364 to chassis number 222500 (approx)
1955: from chassis number 222500 to chassis number 230150 (approx)
1956: from chassis number 230150 to chassis number 233455

Because of the higgledy-piggledy way in which the car/chassis and engine numbers were allocated, possibly the best way of determining where an Austin-Healey 100 comes in the production run is by looking at

the body number. Body numbers were issued from 1 upwards, and body numbers 1 to 20 were used for Warwick-built cars, giving 21 as the first body number for a Longbridge-built car (quoted in the parts list). The body numbers were always prefixed by a four-figure batch number. These batch numbers vary from at least 4021 to 5879 (not all numbers within this span being used). A batch identified by the same batch number may contain anything up to 500 bodies. The highest body number issued is known to have been 14634. The same series of body numbers was used for BN1 and BN2 models; it is thought that the first BN2 body number was 10031, within batch number 5441. The total number of cars made as suggested by the body number series would be 14634.

On the early cars, before the unified car/engine number system was introduced, there should be two plates. The car (chassis) and engine numbers were both stamped on a rectangular white plastic plate found on the scuttle side casing in the footwell on the right-hand side, just in front of the door. In addition, the chassis number (or car number) was found on a plate on the right-hand chassis frame side member alongside the engine (remember that the 'car number' and the 'chassis number' are *always* the same). On the later cars, with the unified number, the 'car/engine number' is found stamped on a plate on the right-hand side of the bulkhead behind the engine.

The engine number is always stamped on a plate on the right-hand side of the cylinder block. The body number is always stamped on a plate on the right-hand side of the bulkhead behind the engine. On this plate, the upper number on the left is the body batch number, and the lower number on the right is the body number itself. The body number, without the batch number, is also stamped in the following locations: on the left-hand side edge of the bonnet about 12in from the back; on the bracket for the prop on the boot lid; and on the back of the four trim strips fitted to the cockpit edges and door tops.

As far as production figures are concerned, the most reliable set of figures seems to be official Austin figures compiled at Longbridge at the time. These figures cover 12-month periods from 1 August one year until 31 July the following year. They are as follows:

1952-53:	94
1953-54:	4424
1954-55:	5348
1955-56:	4748

These give a total of 14614 cars. Now, if we add the 20 early Warwick-built cars, we get a total production of 14634 cars, which exactly equals the body number series (compare above).

If we try to translate these figures into calendar year figures, and comparing with the series of body numbers, we get something like the following figures, including both Warwick- and Longbridge-built cars (totalling 14634 cars again):

1953	1274
1954	5940
1955	4510
1956	2910

But these figures (with the exception of the 1953 total) are only approximations. It is possible to split the BN1 and BN2 models. The BN2 should account for 4604 cars, leaving 10030 BN1 models. This is based on counting the BN2 cars in the production records, and also matches the body number series.

All Big Healeys will have a body number plate like this, found on the bulkhead behind the engine. The first four-digit number is the 'body batch number', followed by the actual body number. These numbers were issued by Jensens. The body number plates are often painted over.

The body number is also stamped in a variety of other locations, such as the bracket on the boot lid where the prop is attached.

It is unfortunately not possible to split the production figure between RHD and LHD, or between home and export, or between different specifications or markets.

Export statistics are only available for 1953 and 1954. Total world exports in these two years were 6032 cars, of which the USA took 3606 cars or 60 per cent. The second biggest market was Australia with 405 cars. Then followed Germany, Canada, France, Belgium/Luxembourg, and Switzerland. These seven markets accounted for more than 84 per cent of all exports. Many cars delivered in Western European markets (such as Germany) or for Personal Export were to North American specification, being bought by US Service Personnel. The likelihood is that at least 75 per cent of all cars were to North American specification. As previously stated, probably less than 10 per cent were RHD cars, for home and export. It seems that there were only around 165 home market BN2 cars, which is about 3.5 per cent.

The BN2 home market figure has been laboriously counted by John Wheatley, a man of infinite patience whose research is behind much of the detailed information contained in this section. He is also responsible for the 100M statistics quoted earlier in the 100M section of this book. Details of 100S production will also be found elsewhere.

COLOUR SCHEMES

The information which is available on the Austin-Healey 100 colour schemes is not as complete as one could wish. While the combinations of paint and interior trim colours are known, complete details of seat piping and hood colours are not known. The colour combinations which were available are listed in the accompanying tables.

The two-tone colour schemes which were offered on the BN2 models, in particular on the 100M version, from late 1955 onwards are listed in table 2 (the first colour listed is the upper body colour).

These tables cover only what one might call the standard colour schemes, and no attempt has been made to list the special order or experimental colours, although

TABLE 1 BN1 & BN2 colours

Paint	Upholstery and trim	Seat piping	Hood	Notes
Healey Grey	Blue	Light Blue-Grey?	?	May be another name for Healey Blue; found only on early cars.
Coronet Cream	Red	Red?	?	1953-54 only.
	Blue	Light Blue-Grey?	?	1953-54 only.
Gunmetal Grey	Red	Red?	?	1953-54; only around 50 cars were built in this colour.
Black	Off-white	Black?	?	1953-54 only.
	Green	Green	Black	BN1 model only.
	Red	Red	Black	Possibly also with red hood.
Healey Blue	Blue	Light Blue-Grey	Blue	—
Old English White	Red	Red	Red	Also with black hood, BN2 only.
	Black	White	Black	—
	Blue	Light Blue-Grey	Blue	Also with black hood, BN2 only.
	Green	Green	?	To 1955 only (BN1 models).
Spruce Green	Green	Green	Green	To Dec 1955.
	Black	White	Black	To Dec 1955.
Carmine Red	Red	Red	Black	To Dec 1955. Also with red hood(?)
	Black	Red	Black	To Dec 1955.
Florida Green	Black	White	Black	From Dec 1955 (BN2).
Reno Red	Red	Red	Black	From Dec 1955 (BN2).
	Black	Red	Black	From Dec 1955.

TABLE 3 Colour codes

Colour name	BMC code number	ICI code number
Black	BK.1	122(?)
Healey Blue	BU.2	2697/2301 M
Florida Green	GN.1	2997
Spruce Green	GN.13	2587
Carmine Red	RD.13	8616/2260
Reno Red	RD.14	3000
Old English White	WT.3	2379/2122
Coronet Cream	none	2583
Healey Grey	?	?
Gunmetal Grey	?	?

TABLE 2 BN2 two-tone colours

Paint	Upholstery and trim	Seat piping	Hood
White/Black	Black	White	Black
Reno Red/Black	Red	Red	Black
Healey Blue/White	Blue	Light Blue-Grey	Blue
Black/Reno Red	Red	Red	Black
Florida Green/White	Black	White	Black

several examples of cars finished in one-off colour schemes are known from the production records (such as lustreen green and claret, or two-tone cars in red and white, or black and pink). There is some confusion over whether Healey Grey was a colour in its own right, or merely Healey Blue under another name. BMC was in the habit of sometimes referring to the same colour by two different names. Healey Blue is the same colour as Ice Blue (metallic), and Old English White is the same colour as Ivory White.

The carpet colour and the boot liners usually matched the colour of the upholstery and trim in general (but both were probably black on cars with off-white trim). The tonneau cover and the fabric on the sidescreens usually matched the hood. The wheels were painted silver. The facia panel was usually painted dark blue on Healey Blue cars, and black on most cars in other colours, while the instrument panel was painted silver.

When paint needs to be ordered for restoration, it is useful to know the BMC paint code number, or a paint manufacturer's number. A list of the BMC and ICI code numbers for Healey 100 colours, as far as they are known, appears in table 3. If more than one ICI code number is listed, it usually indicates that the colour is found in more than one shade. In such cases, care should be exercised in colour matching, and if possible a chip or a sample should be obtained from the paint supplier. The common colours are likely also to be recognised by American paint manufacturers, and other British paint suppliers.

Austin-Healey 100-Six and 3000

Although officially an extra, this adjustable steering wheel is found on most of the 3000 models, as seen here on Roy Standley's Mark I. The gearlever, however, has been shortened, and sports a non-standard wooden knob.

CHASSIS

The basic chassis design of the six-cylinder cars differed very little from the four-cylinder model. The engine mountings were revised, and to give additional space for the six-cylinder engine the radiator was moved in front of the front chassis crossmembers. The upper of these two crossmembers was given a V-shape when seen from the front (or rear). The bracket on the right-hand side of the chassis for the brake master cylinder was deleted.

The wheelbase was lengthened by 2in, from 7ft 6in to 7ft 8in, to accommodate the new rear seats, with the extra length in the area of the door openings. The main difference between the chassis frames for the four-seater models (BN4, BT7 and the later convertibles) and the two-seaters (BN6, BN7) was that the two-seater chassis frames had additional fittings at the rear of the frame to support the batteries. These were missing on the four-seaters and convertibles, where a single 12 volt battery was found in the boot.

The major revision to the chassis frame occurred in 1964 on the Mark III model,

which from chassis number H-BJ8/26705 acquired re-shaped chassis side members. At the point where these passed under the rear axle, they dipped slightly to give additional clearance to the axle on rebound. In combination with the revised rear suspension package the net effect was to improve the ground clearance at the back – always a sore point on the big Healey! The car with these revisions became known as the Phase II model. Another detail change on these cars was that the bracket for attaching the transverse Panhard rod on the right-hand chassis side member was deleted.

FRONT SUSPENSION

Only detail changes occurred to the front suspension on the 100-Six and 3000 models compared to the original 100. However, as the 100-Six was offered with either disc wheels or wire wheels, two different types of wheel hubs were found depending on the type of wheel. Wire wheel hubs went to a coarser thread (from twelve to eight threads per inch) from chassis H-BJ8/26705 in 1964.

Among the other changes affecting the front suspension was the introduction of slightly longer front springs in February 1957 on the BN4 model. On the 3000 Mark I in June 1960, the front coil springs had revised spring rates for better road holding. The spring rates were revised again with the introduction of the BJ7 convertible in 1962. In 1964 on the Phase II Mark III, again from chassis H-BJ8/26705, new front swivel axle assemblies were introduced, which for the first time were handed rather than being identical, and incorporated the brake caliper mountings.

Apart from slight differences to their settings, basically the front shock absorbers were Armstrong hydraulic double-acting lever, type IS9/10RXP. On all models, the castor angle was 2°, the camber angle was 1° and the swivel pin inclination was 6½°.

REAR SUSPENSION

The big change in the rear suspension occurred from chassis H-BJ8/26705 in 1964, the previously-mentioned starting point for the Phase II model of the Mark III. Until then, the cars had seven-leaf rear

A wood-rim steering wheel was at times quoted as an optional extra but the wheel shown here is a Moto-Lita and is probably a non-original fitting. However, this car (Norman Pillinger's BJ7) has the steering wheel hub of cars with non-adjustable steering.

springs, and a transverse Panhard tie rod was fitted. The new rear suspension featured six-leaf springs, the Panhard rod was deleted, and two radius arms were fitted to pedestals on top of the axle casing, running forward to anchorage points in the body structure. The rubber bumpers were relocated to the top of the radius arm pedestals. Also at this time, the arms of the rear shock absorbers were modified to suit, but the type of rear shock absorber was always Armstrong DAS9RXP.

The Phase II six-leaf springs were rather softer than their predecessors as may be gathered from the following details of specification. Seven-leaf springs; laden camber ½in negative; free length, 34.9in. Six-leaf springs; laden camber 1in measured from top leaf; free length, 32⅝in. The laden length of both springs was 36in. The early seven-leaf springs had zinc interleaving, the later six-leaf springs had polypropylene interleaving.

STEERING

The Cam Gears cam and peg steering gear was also basically similar to that of the 100.

In July 1958, from chassis BN6/1995, the steering gear ratio was changed from 14:1 to 15:1 (which they called the new high-efficiency steering gear), and this was then used on all subsequent cars. There were just under three turns lock to lock. For the Abingdon-built cars, we know the exact numbers of right-hand drive and left-hand drive cars built: the total number of right-hand drive cars was 3673, or little more than 7 per cent of total production.

Originally, the BN4 had an adjustable steering column as standard, but on all BN6 cars, on the BN4 from chassis 68960, and all subsequent models, a fixed steering column was standard and the adjustable column an extra. On cars with non-adjustable steering, the column was lengthened by ½in for better clearance to facia in September 1958 (from chassis BN4/70165 and BN6/3395). In September 1961, from chassis 15163 on the 3000 Mark II, cars for export to Germany and Sweden were fitted with a locking steering column. This lock also incorporated the ignition and starter switches. Two alternative types of lock were found, presumably from different suppliers.

The steering wheel was 17in (or 16½in) in diameter, with three four-wire spokes similar to the 100, and also with a black hub and black rim. For cars with non-adjustable steering, two alternative steering wheels were quoted. One was part number AHB6000, of 16½in diameter, made by Bluemels; the other was part number 8G624, of 17in diameter, made by the Clifford Covering Co Ltd of Birmingham. Both of these had large horn pushes, with a sunray or spoke motif to the horn push surround.

The adjustable type steering wheel had a smaller horn push set in a chrome-plated bezel. All horn pushes featured a silver Healey lightning flash with the figure '6' in a round medallion off-set to the right. On the 100-Six the steering wheel flash also had the number 100. The direction indicator switch, of the self-cancelling type (but also different depending on whether the steering was fixed or adjustable), was found on the steering wheel hub above the horn push. A wood-rimmed steering wheel was at times quoted as an extra but very few cars seem to have been so equipped.

The only other change to the steering

gear occurred on the 3000 Mark II model from chassis 19191 in April 1962, when non-lubricated nylon-seated ball joints were introduced for the steering gear connections. The track toe-in was 1/16 to 1/8 in on all models. The turning circle was quoted as 35ft for the 100-Six, and 35ft 7in for the 3000 models.

BRAKES

On the 100-Six, Girling hydraulic drum brakes were found front and rear, with twin leading shoes at the front. The drums were 11in in diameter, with 2¼in wide linings, and a total frictional area of 188sq in. As the brake and clutch pedals were now of the pendant type, the brake master cylinder was mounted on a bracket above the pedal box, being supplied with fluid from a reservoir on the bulkhead on right-hand drive cars; left-hand drive cars had the reservoir on the left-hand vertical support of the bonnet frame. This reservoir also supplied the hydraulic clutch actuation mechanism. The handbrake, found on the right-hand side of the propshaft tunnel, was chrome-plated with a chrome-plated release button and operated a mechanical linkage to the rear brakes. In May 1957, quite early in the BN4 production run, the right-hand seat and carpets were modified to give better clearance for the handbrake. The brake and clutch pedals were rectangular, with studded rubber pads, and curved when seen from the side.

One of the most important modifications on the introduction of the 3000 model in 1959 was that front disc brakes, also made by Girling, were fitted. The discs were 11in in diameter. After about a year in production, the disc brakes had dust covers added to them (see 'Production Changes' for change points by chassis numbers). Otherwise, the braking system was continued largely without change until August 1961, when on the 3000 Mark II model, from chassis 15104, a Girling vacuum servo unit was offered as an optional extra. This became a standard fitting on the Mark III model in 1963, from chassis 25315.

A final modification occurred only on cars exported to France and the Benelux countries, from chassis 41930 in June 1967, when these cars were fitted with a transparent brake fluid reservoir. This necessitated fitting a new separate fluid reservoir for the clutch.

This type of disc wheel was the 'standard' fitting but was found only on a minority of cars. This 3000 Mark I also has the correct type of Road Speed RS5 tyres.

More common is the wire wheel, here shown on Mike Ward's 100-Six. This illustration also clearly shows the feature line running behind the front wheel arch as found on all six-cylinder models.

REAR AXLE

This was the straightforward standard BMC type: a ¾ floating axle in a banjo type case with bolt-on differential carrier, and hypoid bevel gears for the final drive. Two different rear axle ratios were standard fitting on the 100-Six: cars with overdrive had 10/41 (4.1 to 1), cars without overdrive 11/43 (3.909 to 1). On the 3000 ratios were higher, at 11/43 (3.909 to 1) for overdrive cars, 11/39 (3.545 to 1) on cars not fitted with overdrive.

There were no important modifications to the rear axle before the Mark III Phase II model in 1964 at chassis 26705, when the rear axle case was modified to suit the new suspension (please compare the section on rear suspension).

WHEELS & TYRES

From the start of 100-Six production, disc wheels were the standard fitting and wire wheels an optional extra. However, there is little doubt that the great majority of cars, particularly in later years, had wire wheels; in fact these were fitted as standard to North American export cars of the Mark III

model. But the choice of wheels remained open at least to home market buyers until the end of production.

Both disc and wire wheels were originally size 4Jx15. The disc wheels were made by Rubery Owen and had five-stud fixing. They featured eight ventilation holes paired two and two. They were fitted as standard with a chrome-plated hub cap embossed with Austin's Flying 'A' logo. These wheels and hub caps were similar to those found on the Westminster saloon models of the fifties. On the 3000 models, you could theoretically specify Ace Mercury full-width wheel trims as an extra, although it is doubtful that many people ever did.

The wire wheels were supplied by Dunlop, and originally had 48 spokes similar to the 100 wheels. From chassis number 24367 in June 1963, towards the end of the 3000 Mark II Convertible production run, stronger 60-spoke wheels were fitted, size 4.5Jx15. Knock-on hub nuts were fitted, but it became necessary to supply octagonal hub nuts on export cars to Germany and Switzerland from 1958 onwards (possibly first fitted to BN6/2878 in August 1958). Much later, in 1966,

Ian Milne's 1967 Mark III (BJ8) has the 60-spoke wire wheels which are correct on this car. Being a late North American specification model, it also has the octagonal wheel nuts as opposed to knock-ons.

octagonal hub nuts were also fitted to some cars to certain North American destinations. The hub threads were coarser from chassis 26705 (Mark III Phase II model).

Both disc and wire wheels were always finished in silver; the exact paint reference was BMC's Aluminium, code number AL.1.

It may be added here that the paints for the 100-Six and 3000 model chassis components largely followed the pattern set for the 100 models, so unless a specific reference is mentioned in this part of the book, please refer to the first half of the book where the 100 is described in detail.

On a 100-Six with disc wheels, tubeless tyres size 5.90-15 were fitted as standard equipment, but on a car with either wire wheels or overdrive (or both) Dunlop Road Speed tyres (RS4) with inner tubes were fitted, and these could also be specified on their own.

On the 3000 model, Road Speed tyres were fitted as standard, and from June 1960 onwards the RS4 type was replaced by the RS5 (from chassis numbers BT7/10299 and BN7/10309). Whitewall tyres were offered as an optional extra, at least on the Mark II Convertible and Mark III, but possibly also on earlier cars. They were quite common on cars exported to North America. Radial tyres, Dunlop SP.41 size 165HR-15, were another option on the Convertible models, but were primarily found on cars exported to France. Very many cars are now fitted with radial tyres.

Engine

After the formation of BMC in 1952, it became a priority to develop a new medium-sized six-cylinder engine to replace the corporation's three different engines in the 2- to 3-litre bracket – the Morris/Wolseley sohc six, and the Austin and Riley fours. The new design was based

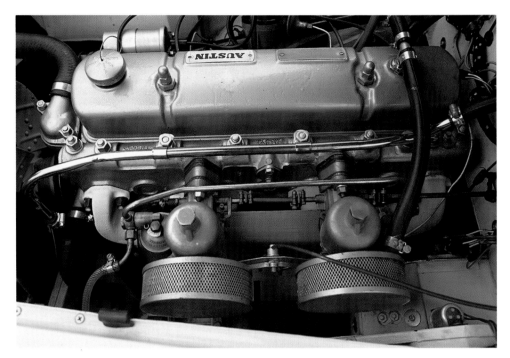

The early Longbridge-built 100-Six BN4 models feature this engine with the so-called four-port head (top). It may more appropriately be called the gallery head, with the inlet manifold integral with the cylinder head. The carburettor dashpots are vertical. This is Roger Bakewell's car.

Another view of Roger Bakewell's early Longbridge-built 100-Six BN4 (above). These air filters are the same type as found on the four-cylinder 100. The red fan shroud on the radiator header tank is correct for most six-cylinder models; the same cannot be said for the red overflow pipe!

on the existing 1.2/1.5-litre Austin/BMC B-series whose stroke of 88.9mm and general lay-out the new engine shared.

The resulting C-series engine was the work of the engineers of Morris Engines Branch in Coventry where these engines were also made. With a bore of 79.4mm, the capacity of the original six-cylinder engine was 2639cc. This engine was introduced in new Austin, Morris and Wolseley saloons in 1954-55. Depending on tuning and carburation it developed between 86 and 95bhp in its original form.

Both block and cylinder head were made from cast iron. The crankshaft ran in four main bearings, originally of the white metal lined type, but changed to the lead-indium type in 1959 soon after the introduction of the 3000 model. Originally there were water passages between all cylinders, but on the 3000 engine, which was bored out to 83.4mm for a resulting capacity of 2912cc, the cylinders were siamesed in three pairs. The camshaft was on the right-hand side of the engine low down, driven by chain from the crankshaft. A timing chain tensioner was fitted, on the 3000 Mark II and later models supplemented by a vibration damper. The vertical in-line overhead valves were activated by push-rods and rockers.

The potential output of the new engine was originally limited by the fact that the cylinder head had a cast-in inlet manifold. The major change which occurred during the production run of the original 100-Six model was the substitution of a much-improved cylinder head with a separate inlet manifold and separate ports for all cylinders, known variously as the six-port or the twelve-port engine. At the same time the valves were increased in size, the compression ratio was raised with the adoption of flat-topped pistons, and larger carburettors were fitted. This engine was installed in some cars from car/engine number BN 4/48863 in October 1957, and in

Moving on to an Abingdon-built 100-Six fitted with the six- (or twelve-) port engine (top). The carburettor dashpots are now inclined, and there is a different type of air filter, which was found also on subsequent models.

The differences are more pronounced when seen from the manifold side: the new separate inlet manifold is clearly visible (above). Note also that the bonnet prop has moved to the right-hand side. The brake/clutch fluid reservoir is at the back of

the engine bay on the right-hand side – compare with the picture of the engine bay of a left-hand drive car later on. The domed cylinder head nuts are not original.

all cars from 52602 in November 1957. The revised engine was found on all Abingdon-built BN4 models as well as the last Longbridge-built cars, and on all BN6 models. (Cars with the more powerful engine were originally launched in the USA as the 100-Six MM, MM for Mille Miglia.)

The next important change was the introduction of the 2912cc engine in the first 3000 (engine type 29D) in March 1959. Another change which occurred early in 3000 production was the substitution of a gear-type oil pump in place of the original Hobourn-Eaton rotary vane type. In March 1961, 3000 Mark II models received engine type 29E fitted with the three carburettor manifold, but in the following year, the Mark II Convertible reverted to a twin carburettor set-up on engine type 29F. In October 1962, French export cars became available with the under-bored 2860cc engine (29FF) to suit French vehicle taxation. The final type of engine was 29K, introduced in October 1963 for the Mark III Convertible, more powerful still with bigger carburettors. For France this became the 2860cc type 29KF, although some later French cars reverted to the 2912cc capacity with engine type 29KFA.

Further details of smaller modifications to the engines will be found in the 'Production Changes' section at the end of this chapter. The table on the facing page gives summarised details of power outputs for the various types of engine.

It is not without interest to realise that what was basically the same car, with not a great deal of extra weight, was given almost 50 per cent more power in the course of development.

The original valve size on the first 100-Six was 1.69in for the inlet valves, and 1.42in for the exhaust valves. On the six-port engine and on all 3000 engines, valves were increased to 1.75in (inlet) and 1.56in (exhaust). With different camshafts used,

There is no obvious visible clue that this is a 3000 Mark I (top). Most of the engine changes over the 100-Six were internal. This car lacks the red fan shroud; the fan is red but should be yellow. The capillary tube to the water temperature gauge should be straight rather than coiled.

It will be evident from this 3000 Mark I (above) that the engine compartment is painted the same colour as the bodywork overall, as may indeed be seen from all of the six-cylinder engine shots. Also, all of the cars featured have the correct type of pressed steel rocker cover, painted the steel dust grey engine colour, with the correct oil filler cap and 'Austin' label.

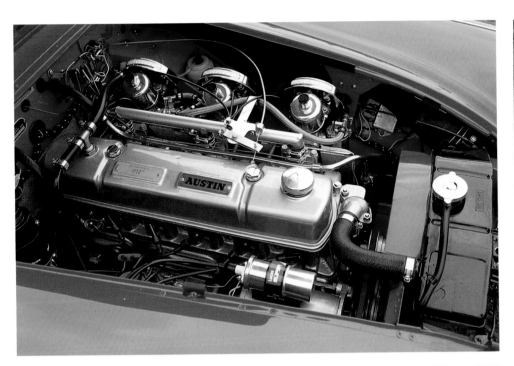

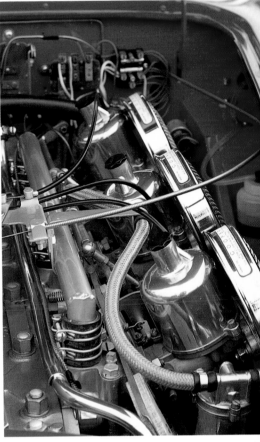

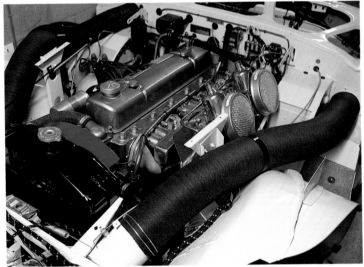

An engine bay with a difference (right)! This Mark I undergoing a rebuild has had the front shroud removed, which gives a much better impression of the lay-out of the air trunking to the heater and fresh-air supply (left and right respectively in the picture).

The engine of Alan Taylor's Mark II is immaculately prepared (top left), although chrome-plated air filters are not original. The ignition coil shown here is a modern replacement. The three-carburettor set-up is rather more complicated than the twin-carburettor system of other models!

The Mark II's three carburettors have the correct black plastic tops, which replaced the brass tops of earlier models (above). This car has its washer bottle in the engine compartment which may not be correct – it would be more typically be set in the parcel shelf under the facia.

Summary of Engine Specification

Model	100–Six early BN4	100–Six, later BN4, all BN6	3000 Mark I, BT7/BN7	3000 Mark II, BT7/BN7	3000 Mark II, BJ7	3000 Mark III, BJ8
Engine type	1C-H	26D	29D	29E	29F	29K
Capacity	2639cc	2639cc	2912cc	2912cc	2912cc	2912cc
Carburation	2 SU H4	2 SU HD6	2 SU HD6	3 SU HS4	2 SU HS6	2 SU HD8
Compression ratio	8.25:1	8.7:1	9:1	9:1	9:1	9:1
Max power (bhp/rpm)	102/4600	117/4750	124/4600	132/4750	131/4750	150/5250
Max torque (lb ft/rpm)	142/2400	149/3000	167/2700	167/3000	158/3000	173/3000

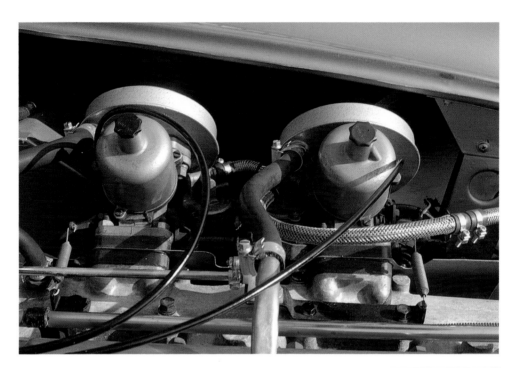

The Mark II Convertible or BJ7 model reverted to twin carburettors, so at first glance appears very similar to the 3000 Mark I. However, the carburettors have slightly shorter dashpots, and are fitted with black plastic tops.

the valve timing on 100-Six and 3000 Mark I models was 5°/45°/40°/10°. The 3000 Mark II, until engine number 29F/2285, had valve timing of 5°/45°/51°/15°. Subsequent Mark II BJ7 models from engine number 29F/2286 had 10°/50°/45°/15°. Finally, for the 29K engine in the Mark III, valve timing was 16°/56°/51°/21°. Engine oil capacity was around 12¾ imperial pints, including the external oil filter (Tecalemit or Purolator). Normal oil pressure while running was 55-60lb for the 100-Six, 50lb at 40mph for the 3000.

The engine was finished in the same metallic grey-green colour as used on the 100, including the bellhousing, dynamo, oil filter, starter motor and engine mountings. The standard rocker cover was made from pressed steel, painted engine colour, and had a twist-lock oil filler cap with a retaining wire on the left. The maker's name label always read simply Austin. A breather pipe was incorporated at the rear of the rocker cover, of T-shape linking up with a breather pipe from the engine side cover. A cast aluminium rocker cover with a quick-release oil filler cap and red Austin-Healey script was a contemporary after-market accessory, not a factory fitting.

Cooling System

Apart from the fact that the radiator had been moved forward in front of the front chassis crossmembers, the cooling system was basically similar to that of the 100

The much fatter carburettor dashpots are immediately evident on the Mark III. From this angle, the new position of the horns may also be seen, while on this model the washer bottle's position under the bonnet is correct.

model. The capacity was 18 imperial pints, with another 2 pints if a heater was fitted (approximately 11 litres). Normal running temperature was 175-195°F (80-90°C) depending on which thermostat was fitted. Originally the thermostat was set to crack open at 158°F (70°C) but in July 1959, from 3000 engine number 29D/3079, this was reduced to 154°F (68°C). On the 3000 Mark II Convertible, from engine number 29F/2592, the original bellows-type thermostat was replaced by a wax thermostat opening at 182°F (83°C). On cars supplied to hot climates, the thermostat might be dispensed with altogether.

The standard fan had four blades, painted yellow (red on some early cars). In

January 1961 a six-blade fan became optional on export cars, and later export cars from 1964 onwards could have eight- or 16-blade fans. There were different types of radiators. The 100-Six radiator had nine gills per inch, and the original 3000 radiator 10 gills per inch. In December 1959, this was replaced by a radiator with 12 gills per inch. A minor change concerned the thermo-capillary pick-up for the water temperature gauge, which was moved from the radiator header tank to the thermostat housing from chassis number BN6/2030 in July 1958. The radiator was always pressurized to 7lb sq in, with an eared cap. The radiator and header tank were black, the fan shroud often red.

The air filters on the Mark III are of a slightly different type, and the front one has been displaced because of the bulkier carburettor. On this left-hand drive car, the brake/clutch reservoir has been moved to the left-hand front shroud support pillar.

The dual exhaust system was found on all Mark III models, with the tailpipes emerging on the right-hand side of the car. This is in fact a replacement exhaust system made of stainless steel, and is missing its clamp. Note that the vertical seam below the tail panel is painted correctly body colour.

A Smiths 3½kw heater was an optional extra but was fitted to the majority of cars, except those exported to hot climates (including a few cars for the southern part of the USA) and a few home market cars. The heater had a fresh-air intake trunk on the right-hand side of the grille, leading to a blower motor on the right-hand front wheel arch. Another length of trunking led back to the heat exchange matrix housed in a black non-gloss finish box under the facia, fitted with footwell outlets and two outlets for the windscreen demisters. On the heater control panel was a central sliding control for regulating the water inlet tap on the heater and thus the temperature. If the knob on the end of this was pulled the blower

would be switched on. The knob on the right regulated the volume of air from the heater, and had to be fully pulled out to shut it off altogether. To obtain the full demisting effect it was necessary to close the shutters for the heater outlets in the footwells. A second knob on the left-hand side of the heater control panel controlled the separate cold air intake through a trunk from the left-hand side of the radiator grille to the left-hand footwell. This ventilation system was fitted to all cars.

The heater took its water from a tap on the rear right-hand side of the cylinder head (the outlet was covered with a blanking plate if a heater was not fitted) and returned it via a copper pipe to the top end of the

bottom radiator hose. A complete kit was made available to fit heaters to cars not originally so equipped.

EXHAUST SYSTEM

Although there were always six exhaust ports, the two centre pairs of exhaust ports were virtually siamesed. The front three and rear three cylinders each had their own exhaust manifold, leading to two down-pipes with flexible sections. There was a single Burgess silencer mounted under the floor on the left-hand side, with dual intakes and outlets, and dual tailpipes running back below the rear axle on the left-hand side. However, it is thought that some early BN4 cars had only a single tailpipe. The exhaust system was mounted in three places – at the front of the silencer, at the rear of the silencer, and behind the rear axle. The manifolds were not painted and the exhaust system itself was black.

In January 1961, from chassis number 13601 (late 3000 Mark I), cars for export to Europe became available with the 'Continental' exhaust system. This had a main silencer of a slightly different pattern, and the tailpipe was split in two sections behind the rear axle. The second section of the tailpipe bent through 90° to a secondary silencer mounted transversely across the tail of the car, with a dual flexible mount on the right-hand side. At the end of the secondary silencer the tailpipes bent through a right angle again, to emerge on the right.

Evidently this was the exhaust system which served as the model for that on the 3000 Mark III model from chassis number H-BJ8/25315 onwards. These cars also had a transverse secondary silencer at the back, with the tailpipe emerging on the right-hand side, but the Mark III exhaust system was completely dualised, with twinned main and secondary silencers. Despite the revised rear suspension package permitting additional axle movement found on Phase II cars from chassis 26705 onwards, no further change to the exhaust system was found necessary. On the BJ8 models, the same exhaust system was found on cars for all markets.

CARBURETTORS AND FUEL SYSTEM

The original 100-Six BN4 model had two SU carburettors of type H4. This indicates that they were 'horizontal' carburettors – the air flow through the carburettor was horizontal, although the bellhousings were vertically mounted – with 4 indicating the 1½in size of the venturi (4 being the number of ⅛ths over an inch of the size). The standard needle was AJ. These carburettors were one reason for the restricted performance of the original engine, so on the revised six-port engine previously described they were replaced by a pair of 1¾in semi-downdraught (mounted at an angle) HD6 carburettors with standard needle CV.

These carburettors were carried forward on the 3000 Mark I models, but for a short interval (July to November 1959, chassis and engine number change points listed in 'Production Changes') they were fitted with an automatic choke device in the form of a thermostatically-controlled auxiliary carburettor, fitted adjacent to the rear carburettor and drawing its fuel supply directly from the float chamber of this. Cars equipped with this device did not have a choke control on the facia, and when the manual choke was re-introduced the choke control was moved from its original hiding place under the facia to the main panel above the heater controls.

The big change on the Mark II model from chassis number 13751 in 1961 was that three carburettors were now fitted, SU type HS4 1½in semi-downdraught, with standard needle DJ. Later versions of these carburettors, from engine number 29E/2995 in November 1961, were fitted with nylon instead of metal floats. Also during the three-carb production run, the

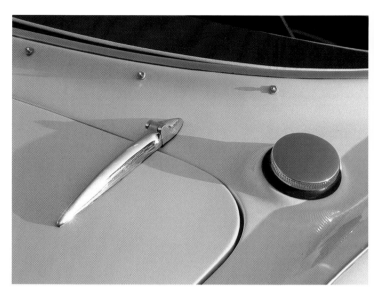

Common to all six-cylinder models is the position of the fuel filler cap on the right-hand side of the rear tonneau panel. This is the standard non-locking type of cap.

carburettor balance pipes were increased in diameter, overflow pipes were improved and the heat shield was covered in asbestos on top as well as on the underside – all in an effort to overcome a problem of fuel vaporising in the rear carburettor.

Although the triple-carburettor set-up gave a valuable increase in power (and also apparently permitted the installation of three Weber carburettors on works cars), they were not totally satisfactory in service as there were usually problems with adjustment and tuning. So on the Mark II Convertible model, type BJ7 with engine type 29F, a reversion was made to the twin-carburettor set-up, now with two HS6 (1¾in) carburettors, standard needle BC. Finally, on the Mark III model in 1964, type BJ8 with engine 29K, a pair of HD8 2in carburettors with standard needle UH were fitted. These are instantly recognisable with their fatter and shorter bellhousings. It is worth noting that whereas the 100-Six and 3000 Mark I carburettors had hexagonal brass tops, on all 3000 Mark II and Mark III models the carburettors had black, knurled plastic tops. On all six-cylinder cars, each carburettor had an individual Coopers pancake type air filter, usually painted engine colour.

The fuel tank was mounted in the boot as before and held 12 imperial gallons (54 litres). However, the fuel filler pipe was now in the front right-hand corner of the tank, leading up to a chrome-plated bayonet fixing filler cap on the right-hand side of the rear tonneau panel. On the 3000 models, a locking filler cap could be specified as a factory-fitted extra.

The SU electric fuel pump was originally mounted behind the heel board on the left-hand side of the car. Originally, the 100-Six had an HP-type fuel pump, but from chassis number BN4/60413, in March 1958, this was replaced by a higher-capacity

LCS-type, also found on all BN6 cars and carried forward on the 3000 models. The fuel pump specification was upgraded in March 1961, and in January 1962 the pump was moved from the left-hand to the right-hand side of the car, to minimise the risk of fuel vaporisation due to heat from the exhaust pipe. Finally, on the Mark III model from chassis number H-BJ8/28225 in August 1964, the new AUF301 fuel pump was introduced, being of a more modern design and of still higher capacity.

TRANSMISSION

A single dry-plate Borg & Beck clutch was fitted to all these cars, but unlike the 100 clutch actuation was now hydraulic, with a shared reservoir for the brake and clutch fluids (except some late export models, compare the section on the braking system). The pendant clutch pedal directly activated the master cylinder fitted on the pedal box, and the clutch operating or slave cylinder was found on the right-hand side below the bell housing. The 100-Six models had a 9in clutch, while on the 3000 models this was increased to 10in. In May 1963, from engine number 29F/4898 on the Mark II Convertible, a new 9½in diaphragm spring type clutch was introduced. The final change occurred on the Mark III from engine number 29K/4108 in October 1964 when the clutch driven plate was reduced in size to 9in.

The standard BMC four-speed gearbox found on the BN2 version of the 100 was carried over on the 100-Six, with the same internal gearbox ratios. The gearlever was chrome-plated, the knob a black ball with an engraved white pattern. The overdrive ratio was also unchanged. As previously indicated there were two different rear axle ratios depending on whether or not overdrive was fitted, and so we obtain the following table of 100-Six gear ratios:

	INTERNAL RATIOS	OVERALL RATIOS without overdrive	OVERALL RATIOS with overdrive
First	3.076	12.02	12.61
Second	1.913	7.48	7.84
Third	1.333	5.21	5.47
Third o/d	1.037	n/a	4.25
Fourth	1.00	3.909	4.1
Fourth o/d	0.778	n/a	3.19
Reverse	4.17	16.30	17.1

On the 3000 Mark I model from the beginning of production, the internal gearbox ratios were revised, and in conjunction with the altered rear axle ratios produced the following sets of ratios:

	INTERNAL RATIOS	OVERALL RATIOS without overdrive	OVERALL RATIOS with overdrive
First	2.93	10.386	11.453
Second	2.053	7.277	8.025
Third	1.309	4.640	5.116
Third o/d	1.073	n/a	4.195
Fourth	1.00	3.545	3.909
Fourth o/d	0.822	n/a	3.205
Reverse	3.78	13.400	14.776

These ratios did not last long, as in February/March 1960 the gearbox ratios were revised yet again, coinciding with a major improvement to the gearbox as the entire gearcluster was made more rigid. This occurred on cars with overdrive from engine number 29D/10897 (gearbox number 6656) and cars without overdrive from engine number 29D/11342 (gearbox number 1177). The resultant ratios were:

	INTERNAL RATIOS	OVERALL RATIOS without overdrive	OVERALL RATIOS with overdrive
First	2.88	10.209	11.257
Second	2.06	7.302	8.052
Third	1.31	4.643	5.120
Third o/d	1.074	n/a	4.198
Fourth	1.00	3.545	3.909
Fourth o/d	0.822	n/a	3.205
Reverse	3.72	13.1	14.541

It will be noted that these revisions affected first, second and reverse gears, and were relatively minor. Apart from other smaller gearbox changes listed in 'Production Changes', the next important change occurred in November 1961 when the 3000 Mark II models were given a new gearbox design with top rather than side selectors, and it became possible to have a true centre gearchange with a short, vertical lever rather than the former side gearchange with the cranked lever. This modification took place from engine number 29E/2246, chassis numbers BT7/15881 and BN7/

The four-seater models and the Convertibles have a single 12-volt battery on the right-hand side of the boot, with the master switch just behind the battery. This is a 100-Six – you can tell because it has the now much sought-after conical covers to the rear reflectors, unique to this model among Austin-Healeys.

16039. The ratios were not changed, however.

The final revised set of gear ratios was introduced on the Mark III model from commencement in October 1963; otherwise this model took over the existing gearbox without major change. On the Mark III models the following ratios were found:

	INTERNAL RATIOS	OVERALL RATIOS without overdrive	OVERALL RATIOS with overdrive
First	2.637	9.348	10.308
Second	2.071	7.341	8.095
Third	1.306	4.629	5.105
Third o/d	1.071	n/a	4.188
Fourth	1.00	3.545	3.909
Fourth o/d	0.82	n/a	3.207
Reverse	3.391	12.021	13.255

Apart from the overdrive ratio being altered from the 100-Six to the 3000 models, the overdrive was not subject to any great changes. The Hardy Spicer propshaft was similar to the one found on the 100 model, and was not subject to any important change during the life of the six-cylinder models.

ELECTRICAL EQUIPMENT AND LAMPS

Lucas electrical equipment was fitted. A major modification necessary on the four-seater BN4 model had been the relocation of the battery to make room for the rear seats. On this and subsequent four-seater cars a single 12-volt battery was fitted on the right-hand side of the boot, with a master switch immediately behind it. The BN4 had a GTW9A battery (GTZ9A was the dry-charged variety for export cars), the

On the two-seater models (this is a 3000 Mark I) the two six-volt batteries are accessible through a trap door in the tonneau – an arrangement similar in principle to that found on the four-cylinder 100 models.

The headlamps and side lamps (incorporating flashing indicators) of the 100-Six and most of the 3000 models were of the same type, and were also found on the original four-cylinder cars. This 3000 Mark I has been fitted with a badge bar and a pair of auxiliary lamps – both of the correct type as period accessories.

BT7 and later convertible models had a BT9A battery (or BTZ9A if dry-charged). Both had a 58 AH capacity.

The BN6 and BN7 two-seater models retained the two six-volt batteries, type SLG11E (dry-charged SLGZ11E) located on shelves on the chassis, accessible through a trapdoor in the tonneau floor behind the seats. On two-seater cars the battery master switch was on the left-hand side of the boot. Battery capacity was the same as on the four-seater models. All cars were wired positive to earth; while the wiring was normally covered in colour-coded plastic, the main harness had a braided cloth cover.

The dynamo was type C45PV5 on the 100-Six, C45PV6 on the 3000 Mark I and II, and C42PVC on the Mark III. The starter motor was type L3M418G on all cars. Both were finished in engine colour. The original distributor was type DM6A, but during the 3000 Mark II Convertible production run it was changed to type 25D6 (from engine number 29F/3563) with pre-tilted contact breakers. This was then carried forward to

the Mark III model. The ignition coil was type HA12 and was always fitted with a clamp on top of the dynamo. Champion 14mm ¾in reach sparking plugs were fitted, with a plug gap of .025in. The original 100-Six BN4 was fitted with NA8 plugs and ignition timing was quoted as 5° ATDC, subsequently revised to 6° BTDC. The six-port engines on later BN4 and all BN6 cars had N5 plugs, and the timing was also 6° BTDC. The 3000 Mark I was at first fitted with N3 plugs, but in June 1959 the N5 type was recommended as an alternative for town running. N3 was still preferred for high speed motoring. The ignition timing on these models was 5° BTDC. On the Mark II model, the choice of N3 or N5 plugs was still quoted, but ignition timing was revised to 12° BTDC. On the BJ7 Convertible model, Champion UN12Y were later specified; they were also fitted to the Mark III model and were recommended as replacements on earlier models. Mark III ignition timing was 10° BTDC (static) and 15° BTDC

(stroboscopic). The firing order was 1, 5, 3, 6, 2, 4 on all cars.

The control box was type RB106/2 until replaced on the 3000 Mark III model by type RB340. The separate fuse box type SF6 (4FJ on Mark III) held two fuses, of 50amp and 35amp capacity. On later Mark III cars, an in-line fuse of 10amp was fitted to the numberplate lamp circuit. A starter solenoid switch type ST950 was fitted.

The basic type of headlamp was F700 with convex block-type lenses, except on North American cars which had sealed beam lamps (fitted at the factory from July 1959 onwards, if not earlier). Depending on market destination, export cars had lamps dipping to the left, vertically, or to the right. In April 1960 headlamps with assymmetrical dip were introduced for the first time, beginning with cars for Sweden, later probably fitted to most European cars. French cars were fitted with yellow bulbs. There were some modifications to the headlamps on the Mark III models which were fitted with the so-called Mark X

Only on the 3000 Mark III in March 1965 were lighting arrangements changed (apart from certain earlier export cars). At the rear (right), separate indicator lamps with amber lenses took the place of the reflectors in the pods above the rear lamps. Both the indicator lamp and the rear/stop lamps now had the larger plastic lenses. The reflectors were banished to brackets on the bumper as seen here.

In terms of lighting, the rear aspect was not changed on the original six-cylinder models: this is the 3000 Mark I (above). On this model, the reflectors had lost the conical covers found on the 100-Six.

headlamps from September 1965 onwards.

Originally combined sidelamps and flashing indicators were fitted, type 594 with white glass lenses and chrome-plated rims. In September 1961 (chassis 15163) cars for Germany and Sweden became equipped with separate indicator lamps (also originally type 594) with amber lenses, and in March 1965 the separate indicator lamps became the standard fitment on all cars, from chassis 31336 (and a few earlier cars). A larger sidelamp type 692 with a flatter, conical plastic lens had been fitted from chassis 26705 (the Phase II model of the Mark III) from May 1964 onwards. The flasher unit was type FL5.

The original stop/tail lamp was also type 594 and also incorporated the direction indicators. Again in September 1961, German and Swedish cars acquired separate rear indicators with amber lenses, taking

the place of the reflectors in their pods on the tonneau panel above the rear lamps. At chassis 26705 the larger type 692 rear lamp with plastic lens, similar to the new front sidelamps, was fitted. This later type of lamp lacked the chrome-plated bezel found on the original side and rear lamps. The separate rear indicators became a standard fitting on all cars in March 1965 (compare above). On six-cylinder cars before the introduction of separate rear indicators, the rear reflectors were mounted in the pods above the rear lamps, as on the 100 model – but *only* the 100-Six had conical covers fitted over the reflectors. These covers have been reported in red, amber or clear plastic. On cars fitted with separate indicators, the rear reflectors were fitted on brackets above the bumper to the outside of the rear lamps.

The numberplate lamp was type 467/2 with a chrome-plated housing. Originally

There were also changes at the front in March 1965 (above). There were now separate side lamps (white lens) and flashing indicator lamps (amber lens) at the front, and these lamps were the larger type with plastic lenses introduced from the start of the Mark III Phase II model in 1964.

Of all the six-cylinder models, the two-seaters came closest in looks to the original 100 – but the grille and bonnet were immediate giveaways. This 3000 Mark I has, it must be admitted, the side flashes on the wings fitted the wrong way round. Also, the front number plate should be hung under the bumper, with a backing plate on home market cars.

it had a single bulb only but from chassis 13531 (3000 Mark I, December 1960) it was fitted with two bulbs. Some later European export cars were fitted with two numberplate lamps, each with one bulb. They looked the same but had different internals and bulbs.

The horns specified on the 100-Six and 3000 Mark I models were HF1748, on Mark II and Mark III models 9H. The earlier type horns were fitted to the front crossmember, the later type on the right-hand side of the engine compartment just below the bonnet. The windscreen wiper motor was type DR2 until replaced by type DR3A late in the Mark II Convertible production run (body 60792 in August 1963).

As on the 100, the wiper motor was located on a bracket under the scuttle on the left-hand side of the car. A windscreen washer was always standard equipment on the six-cylinder models, originally a Trafalgar with a glass reservoir, but during the 100-Six production run changed to a Tudor with a plastic bottle. Both had manual pump actuation. The reservoir was fitted in a holder set in the parcel shelf under the facia on the passenger side, except on the Mark III where it was found in the

engine compartment. Most cars had two washer jets on the scuttle, but some 100-Six cars had only one central jet with two nozzles.

BODY AND BODY TRIM

In general construction and design the body differed little from the 100 body. Aluminium continued to be used for the front shroud and rear tonneau panels, with the remainder of the skin panels in steel. The additional wheelbase length of the six-cylinder cars was accommodated by wider doors, so the front and rear wings were of similar dimensions to the 100. Two important identification points were that all six-cylinder models had external door handles, and the body swage line was continued in front of the side flash, with a hockey stick return separate from the front wheel arch, running parallel with the wheel arch down to the sill. This meant that on two-tone cars the upper body colour was found on the edge of the wheel arch all the way round. On the six-cylinder cars, the piping below the headlamps was silver, with a round bead cross-section.

On four-seater cars and later on convertibles, the rear tonneau panel was cut

back to make room for the occasional rear seats. Two-seater cars had a much deeper rear tonneau panel similar to that of the 100. The bonnet was longer on the six-cylinder cars, coming further forward towards the grille at the front. It was now hinged at the rear, with a remote bonnet lock control under the facia. Two bonnet safety catches were fitted, one at each side towards the front. The manual bonnet prop was on the left-hand side on early BN4 models, but on later BN4s, BN6s and all 3000 models it was on the right-hand side. The bonnet had a bulge for additional radiator clearance. At the front, the bulge was finished with a small air intake with a chrome-plated finisher and grille. On the 100-Six and 3000 Mark I, this had three vertical bars with one horizontal bar between them, while on 3000 Mark II and Mark III models an all-vertical bar pattern was found. Some 100-Six cars had a central crease in the bonnet bulge, never found on the 3000.

Compared to the 100, the radiator grille was bigger and wider, and of a more pronounced oval shape. The 100-Six and 3000 Mark I models had a grille of horizontal wavy bars, of a pattern found on many Austin saloon cars of the late fifties and early sixties. The 3000 Mark II and

The major redesign came with the introduction of the Convertible model – this is a late Mark III. The new windscreen, the quarterlights, the added panel at the door top and the new hood are all evident. This car, being a North American export model, has a special type of rear numberplate bracket and lamp.

The new windscreen was less apparent in front view. The vertical bar radiator grille was introduced from the start of Mark II production in 1961. This Mark III Convertible has been fitted with a door-mounted mirror which is not correct – the external mirrors available as extras at the time were wing-mounted.

The wavy line grille bars found on the 100-Six and 3000 Mark I (left) were of a pattern common to most Austin saloons of the late 1950s. On the 100-Six the original lightning flash badge of the 100 had this small roundel with the figure '6' added to it. Through the grille the single X-bracing in front of the radiator is visible.

Common to all 3000 models is this additional boot lid badge (left) with the figures '3000' on a lightning flash.

The '3000' lightning flash badge is found on the radiator grille only on the 3000 Mark I model (above). The Mark I grille was unchanged from the original 100. This style of bonnet air intake was found on the 100-Six and 3000 Mark I models.

The Mark III badge was similar to the Mark II except for the obvious alteration (left). Note the lack of a hyphen between Austin and Healey. This type of badge was originally finished with vitreous enamel but later the background was simply painted red.

The frontal aspect of the Mark II (above) was considerably changed by the new vertical bar radiator grille, with matching vertical bars to the bonnet air intake. The grille no longer carried a badge, but there was a new type of badge above the grille, with a supplementary badge reading '3000 Mk II'. This style of grille and badge was carried over on the Convertible model.

Mark III models received a new vertical bar grille, with a 'kink' about halfway down the bars. Finishers were fitted above and below the grille, on the early cars with a much deeper section to the top finisher, on Mark II and III cars of more equal proportions all round. The top finisher on the 100-Six and 3000 Mark I was polished stainless steel, while the bottom finisher was chrome-plated. On Mark II and III cars, the entire surround was chrome-plated .

The 100-Six had the Healey lightning flash badge on the left-hand side of the grille (on the right if you look from the front) with the number 100 picked out in red, and the number 6 set in a round medallion with a red background.

The winged badge with the red Austin-Healey script mounted between the bonnet and the radiator grille was carried over from the 100 to the 100-Six and 3000 Mark I. On the 3000 Mark I, a new radiator grille badge was fitted, with the number 3000 in red on the lightning flash. On the Mark II and Mark III models, the grille badge was deleted, and a new badge was fitted above the grille, with the 'Austin Healey' script on a red background and a winged surround, and a smaller badge below reading '3000 MkII' or '3000 MkIII'. On this later style of badge, 'Austin Healey' was *not* hyphenated. The red background of these badges was vitreous enamel at first, later simply painted.

A significant difference between the four- and six-cylinder models was that the latter always had a fixed windscreen, as shown here on the 100-Six but found also on the 3000 Mark I and II models. The shape, however, was not unlike that of the original 100 windscreen.

On the Mark II Convertible the 'wrap-around' windscreen was introduced (above), with chrome-plated as opposed to body-colour pillars and a much wider chrome-plated frame. Note the swivelling quarterlights and the chrome-plated capping pieces added to the door tops.

This detail shot of the 3000 Mark I shows how the scuttle panel behind the windscreen is covered in Vynide to match the facia covering (and the upholstery/trim colour), while the demister outlets are painted to match the Vynide colour. The edging strip above the facia was not an aluminium strip as on the 100, but a padded roll on a wood base, again covered in Vynide.

The major modification that occurred during the six-cylinder production run was the introduction of the convertible type of body in 1962 for the BJ7 (Mark II) and later BJ8 (Mark III) models. The loose sidescreens of the earlier cars were now replaced by wind-down door windows, with swivelling quarterlights in chrome-plated frames at the front (the drop glasses were unframed). A deep chrome-plated finisher was fitted to the top of the door skin panel, to bring the door top up to a higher and more horizontal line. The internal door construction was modified to accommodate the window winding mechanism.

The windscreen was also modified on the convertibles. The original windscreen with its body colour pillars and chrome-plated frame resembled that of the 100, but was fixed in place. Apparently the folding windscreen of the 100 was dispensed with as it was considered to cause too many windscreen breakages to the detriment of Austin's warranty costs. The windscreen introduced on the convertible models was rather more curved, particularly at the sides, and was commonly known as the wrap-around screen. It had an all chrome-plated frame. Laminated glass was always used, but some of the late American export cars in 1967 were fitted with improved quality high impact resistant glass.

At the rear of the car, the boot lid of the 100-Six only carried the Austin-Healey script badge as found on the 100, but on the 3000 models this was supplemented by a lightning flash carrying the 3000 numbers in red, similar to the radiator grille badge found on the 3000 Mark I. The locking boot handle and its escutcheon were carried over from the 100 and were not subject to any change. On all six-cylinder cars the boot lid had a manual prop, attached in the bottom left-hand corner of the lid. Another external identification point of a six-cylinder model was the fuel filler cap on the right of the tonneau panel.

The external door handles fitted to the early 100-Six BN4 had a key-operated lock on the left-hand side, but this was soon deleted and plain pull handles were found

Compared to the 100, the six-cylinder cars have bumpers of a deeper and flatter section, with a wider central groove (left). The overriders are virtually identical. Here seen on a 100-Six, the bumpers were similar also on all subsequent models.

The boot lid handle and escutcheon were unchanged from the 100 to the six-cylinder models. The lock barrel should be flush with the edge of its surround, not recessed as seen here. The conical reflector covers tell us that this is a 100-Six, which simply has the Austin-Healey script on the bootlid without any other badging.

Only the early 100-Six models had this door handle with an external lock, and only on the left-hand door (the right-hand door had a plain non-locking handle). Apparently these handles came from the Jowett Javelin! Shown here stripped, the handle should be chrome-plated.

on all models thereafter, until chassis 26705 in 1964 when the Mark III Phase II model was fitted with push-button door handles with a key-operated lock on both doors. On cars with external key locks, the same key was used for the ignition, the door locks and the boot lock; the exception to this rule being export cars fitted with steering locks which had a different key for this. All cars had an oval depression behind the door handle for finger clearance, and a small bulge was pressed out of the doorskin panel to continue the line of the door handle forward. Cars with pull handles had small rubber bumpers under the free ends of the handles.

The bumpers looked similar to those of the 100 but were in fact of a different, more rounded section. Overriders were fitted front and rear, with black plastic piping between bumper and overrider. The bumper brackets were T-shaped and were painted black. At the front they passed below the front panel, at the rear they passed through rubber grommets in the tail panel. Full-width bumper support bars were not fitted. A body-colour front apron panel was found behind the front bumper on all models, except on the BN6 model prior to chassis 4022 in November 1958.

Black-painted numberplate backing plates were fitted to cars supplied in the home market. On export cars there was an adjustable bracket for a rear number-plate, also sometimes supporting the numberplate lamp, with some variation

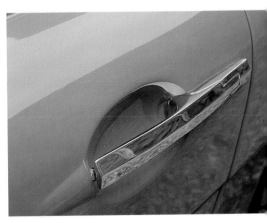

This is the plain non-locking handle soon standardised on both doors and then used until a push-button handle with external key locks on both sides was introduced on the Mark III Phase II in 1964.

depending on model, market and time of manufacture. Other cars had the numberplate lamp on a bracket inside the bumper bar.

Another area where the body construction was modified from the 100 was in front of the radiator, which was moved forward on the six-cylinder cars. The cross bracing between the chassis and the bonnet locking platform was therefore also moved forward, and there was only a single 'X'.

Although touted by Austin as a four-seater (and indeed always referred to in this way as a matter of convenience), the BN4 100-Six was still really only comfortable as a two-seater, with the rear seats at the most suitable for the occasional carriage of small children. The contrast colour seat piping was found on all models until the 3000 Mark III.

No central dividing panel was fitted, but in August 1957 air deflectors were added to each side of the radiator grille on the 100-Six from chassis BN4/47184.

The chrome-plated flashes were still found on the front wings, and were fitted with the thicker end towards the back (they are fitted the wrong way round on one car photographed for this book). The small air vents hidden behind the wing flashes on the 100, however, were deleted on the six-cylinder cars. No standard factory car ever had air outlets in the front wings behind the wheel arches, but they were found on the works rally and race cars, and have often been added to cars by subsequent owners, especially in the USA where they help to overcome the Healey's perennial foot-frying tendencies.

The optional-extra fibreglass hard top was available for the 100-Six and the 3000 Mark I and II models (except the Mark II Convertible). Two different hard tops of slightly different dimensions were found on two-seater and four-seater models, but the same hard tops were used right through the production period. The hard tops featured a large, curved rear window made of plexiglas. Inside the rear window were two vertical support brackets. The hard top was fitted with spigots into sockets behind the door openings, and was secured with hooks under the rear tonneau rail and with toggle catches to the windscreen frame. For hard top colours and colour combinations, please see the colour list. Replacement hard tops, and hard tops supplied for after-market purposes, were normally finished in primer.

INTERIOR TRIM, BOOT AND HOOD

The interior remained basically the same from the start of 100-Six production to the end of the Mark II Convertible. The Mark III had a different interior. In the following, the first group will be referred to as the early cars, and the Mark III will be described on its own.

Two bucket seats were fitted, with hinged squabs folding forward. During the 100-Six production run, seat construction was changed, metal pans replacing wooden bases. On the early cars the seats were very similar to the 100, having central panels with five flutes to cushion and squab, surrounded by wide edge bolsters. The centre panels and the edges of the seats had piping in a contrast colour (except the black seats on a Mark II Convertible in British Racing Green, which had black piping). The seats were upholstered in leather on the wearing parts and the cushion edges, with Vynide on non-wearing parts including the backs of the squabs. Both seats could be adjusted with a slide on the outside seat runner.

On four-seaters and convertibles, small rear seat pans were carved out of the tonneau floor panel. Each individual seat pan had four flutes. The common rear seat squab had ten vertical flutes across the car.

While the front seats were still upholstered in leather on the 100-Six, and indeed on the 3000 before the Mark III model, the rear seat pans and back rest were covered in Vynide. Part of the hoodframe is still visible, in the recesses either side of the rear seat, even when the hood is stowed away. The sockets for the hoodframe are just in front of the feet of the frame. The hard top mounting point can just be seen at the bottom of the picture.

The two-seater (here a 3000 Mark I) has a totally different style of armrest compared to the four-seater (see the earlier picture of a 100-Six interior). This Pacific Green car has the correct grey trim with green piping and green carpets. However, the edge binding around the gearlever should probably be green rather than grey.

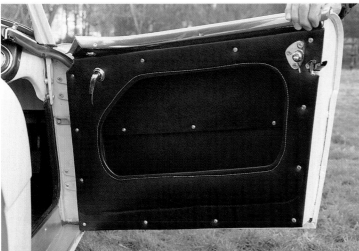

The 100-Six door trims were similar to the 100, but the pull cord was replaced by an internal handle at the front of the door. As the car also had external handles, the interior handle at the rear of the door was deleted. This car has an early type of sidescreen mounting point at the rear, with a butterfly nut. The front sidescreen mounting point was still in a socket in the door thickness, just visible above the handle.

The patterned aluminium tread plates and lock pillar cover plates are also reminiscent of those found on the 100, but this 3000 Mark I is fitted with a black rubber seal all the way around the door opening, as well as an inner Furflex seal.

This squab folded forward to allow stowage of the hood behind it. The interior rear seats and trim panels were finished in Vynide (leathercloth) to match the colour of the front seat upholstery.

The door casings were very simple, trimmed in Vynide with just a row of stitches round the door pocket. The inside of the pocket was similarly trimmed in Vynide. There was an internal door handle at the front, chrome-plated with a chrome-plated escutcheon. Apart from the outer door seal in black rubber, there was also an inner door seal. On early BN4 cars this was black rubber, but on the BN6, later BN4 cars (from chassis 68960) and 3000 cars it was colour-coded Furflex to match the trim. The exception to this rule were the few cars with yellow trim, which had black Furflex strips. The Furflex strips were visible to the front and the rear of the door opening but disappeared under a patterned aluminium sill tread plate. The lock pillars were covered by similar aluminium plates. The Mark I Convertible naturally had different door trims and fittings, described below.

The floor was covered in hessian-backed Karvel carpet, laid over rubberised underfelt and held in place by press studs. The carpet extended also to the area under the seats, the heelboard, the bulkhead and to the gearbox extension. The propshaft tunnel was also covered in carpet. It had a small armrest between the seats, trimmed in leather with three flutes, and with contrast-

The biggest re-design of the Big Healey interior came with the Mark III (BJ8) Convertible. The new wooden facia, and the Ambla-covered seats are the most striking features, but note also the centre console. This late Phase II car has the long fixed armrest. This American car has a number of accessories probably supplied in the USA when it was new, including the radio, the lap seat belts, and the rubber overmat with the Austin-Healey badge. All interesting and legitimate period items.

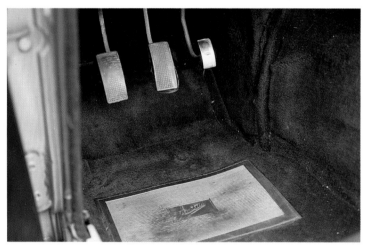

The footwells and the pedal arrangements are similar on all six-cylinder models (left). This is a Mark III, and as is obvious it is a left-hand drive car. The dip switch is just out of sight immediately to the left of the clutch pedal. The 'Austin' script in the heel mat can be clearly seen in this illustration.

colour piping to match the seats. There was a rubber heel mat set in the carpet on the driver's side with an 'Austin' script. The carpet did not have bound edges, except around the gearlever aperture. An ash tray with a chrome-plated swivel lid was set in the tunnel in front of the armrest.

Found under the passenger's side of the facia, the carpet-covered parcel shelf with its Vynide-trimmed edge was similar to that on the 100 but now had a hole in it for the windscreen washer bottle. On the left-hand side under the facia was the separate fresh-air intake, fed by trunking from the radiator grille, and with a shutter adjustable from the heater control panel on the facia. There were aluminium trim strips to the door tops and the front edge of the tonneau panel at the rear of the cockpit. The trim

strip above the facia was padded with rubber on a wood base, and was covered in Vynide to match the facia. On four-seater cars the gap between the tonneau panel and the rear seat squab was filled by a Vynide-covered banana-shaped panel which formed the top of the hood stowage box and was an integral part of the squab assembly.

Not many changes affected the interior but it is worth mentioning that in December 1957, from BN4/52704 (body 7320), the bulkhead panel was strengthened around the gearbox aperture to reduce scuttle shake.

From the introduction of the Mark II model, chassis 13751 in March 1961, seat belt mounting points were added to the body structure, on the rear wheel arches, to

The Mark II convertible (BJ7) model had completely changed door trims, with handle, window winder and door pull all borrowed from the Austin Farina saloon range. The interior handle, however, should point upwards. There is still a very narrow pocket in this door trim.

each side of the propshaft tunnel, and in the floor by the sills at the back of the doors. It was possible to add seat belt mounting points to the earlier 100-Six and 3000 Mark I cars, and a conversion kit was available for this purpose. Seat belts were normally dealer installed; the recommended type supplied by BMC was the Kangol Magnet static three-point type. On a few cars notably later cars supplied direct by the factory for personal export, seat belts were installed at the factory before delivery. Seat belts must now be fitted to all cars in the UK manufactured in or after July 1964 (for practical purposes, on all Mark III models). Some cars sold in the USA had American-made seat belts installed locally.

The new gearbox introduced in November 1961 brought with it a new gearbox cover in fibreglass with a turret round the base of the gearlever, with various attendant changes to trim panels and carpets. And as the 3000 Mark II Convertible model had wind-down windows, it was fitted with new door casings. These still retained a vestige of the original door pocket, with four lines of stitching inside the 'pocket' area. A new type of interior door handle was fitted. There was a window winder, with a black plastic knob, and a pull-handle at the top of the door. All of this door furniture was borrowed from contemporary Austin 'Farina' saloon models.

The Mark III model had a rather different interior. The seats were now upholstered in Ambla as standard. The centre panels now had six flutes to the cushion and squab, with an embossed pattern of small squares. There was a half-moon shaped panel at the top of the central flutes in the seat squabs. Contrast piping was no longer used. Ambla-trimmed seats had piping in 'imitation chrome' which can best be described as piping of clear plastic with a twisted chrome centre. If the optional leather upholstery was specified, piping was in the main seat colour.

The rear seats had ten flutes to each seat pan, also in patterned Ambla. The rear seat squab and the rear quarter side trim panels had a pattern of squares. The rear seat squab still folded forward, but now could now be unfolded (as it was in two hinged pieces) and was then converted into a carpet-covered luggage platform. When unfolded it was locked in place with what I call bathroom door slides, fitting into brackets on the side panels. The Mark III door casings were simplified, losing the shallow

The BJ8's still very occasional rear seats also feature Ambla trim (left). The piping on this car has yellowed with age. Note the pattern of squares to the back rest and the side panels. Also, this Phase II car has the bottom corner of the side panel cut away in the area of the mounting point for the rear axle radius arm.

A novel feature on the Mark III was the way in which the rear seat backrest could not only be folded forward, but could be unfolded to make a handy carpet-covered luggage platform (left, above and below). The 'bathroom slides' were then secured in brackets on the side panels (above), which have a pattern of squares. The 'pimple' to the left in the picture above is the third seat belt mounting point, not in use on this car which has American-type lap belts rather than diagonal three-point type belts, which would be normal on cars sold in the UK. Also seen are the embossed Ambla used on the seat and the special type of seat piping.

The boot of the 100-Six four-seater is very full of spare wheel and battery. Unlike the 100, which had an automatic boot prop, the prop on the six-cylinder models was manual. Note that the fuel pipe is boxed-in for protection on the four-seater cars.

On the Convertible models such as this 3000 Mark III (below), the boot differs little from the original four-seater, but this car has what is felt to be the original battery cover, missing on the four-seater illustrated in the picture above.

With the exception of the red-handled screwdriver which is strictly non-original, this is a fair example of the tool kit on a six-cylinder car – rather sparser than that of the four-cylinder 100. As this 3000 Mark I runs on disc wheels, there is a wheel brace instead of the wheel hammer.

The Mark III (BJ8) model door trim completely lost the pocket. This picture also shows the shape of the frameless drop window glass. The door casing was now fitted with clips rather than visible screw heads – cheaper and simpler in production at the time but now more of a headache to the restorer.

pockets of the Mark II Convertible, with a featureless central panel surrounded by piping. The door handles were not changed. An important feature on the Mark III was a centre console which covered the propshaft tunnel and linked up with the facia. It was covered in Vynide with a chrome-plated edge beading. There was a large rubber grommet round the base of the gearlever. Originally there was quite a short armrest at the rear of the console, and this swung up to reveal a small cubbyhole. However, on the Phase II Mark III (from chassis 26705 in May 1964) this was replaced by a longer, fixed armrest without a cubbyhole.

The boot was lined with felt-backed Armacord panels. There was a protective shield round the fuel filler pipe on four-seaters and convertibles. Originally colour-coded to match the carpets on the early BN4 cars, the boot liners became uniformly black from chassis BN4/68960 as well as on BN6 cars and all 3000 models. On the four-seater the spare wheel was found to the left

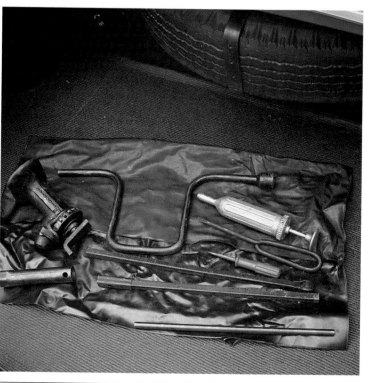

On the two-seaters, the spare wheel position was similar to that of the original 100, but the spare wheel was now in the centre of the car rather than off-set. This carpet spare wheel bag has caused some dissension among the experts – the only way to escape the dilemma is to say that it is original, but some cars had equally original spare wheel bags in vynide!

The hood colours were black, blue or grey, and the hood material was PVC-covered fabric. An aluminium trim strip was found on the front of the hood of 100-Six and 3000 two- and four-seaters. There was a one-piece clear plastic rear window. The hood frames were normally painted grey. The hoods were attached by toggle catches to the windscreen pillars, while at the rear a hood plate was secured by two brackets on the tonneau panel on the two-seaters, with a turn-buckle and two Tenax fasteners either side. On the four-seaters the hood fabric was secured with a row of Tenax fasteners across the car.

While the two-seaters had a two-bow hood frame, the four-seater models had a three-bow frame. The early BN4 hood frame was attached to the sides of the cockpit in sliding channels but was substantially revised from chassis number 68960. When raised, the main bow of the revised hood frame fitted into sockets (as did the BN6 and 3000 hood frames), one on each side behind the door. To lower the hood, the frame had to be lifted clear of these sockets, and the hood cover pulled clear of the frame. The collapsed hood frame and the folded cover were then stored in the hood well behind the rear seat squab of the four-seater, while on the two-seater the hood was simply stored behind the seats, with the main hood frame bow secured by stirrups low down on the rear quarterpanels. Raising or lowering the hood on the early cars was a somewhat difficult operation.

By contrast with a four-seater boot, the two-seater has an unprotected fuel pipe (right). The boot is much roomier with spare wheel and batteries being out of the way. The Armacord boot mat and liners are black on most cars, with the exception of the early BN4 models where they were colour-coded to the interior trim.

A useful extra little cubbyhole under the boot mat on the 3000 Mark I (below).

on the boot floor, held in place by a tie-rod and a leather strap, and the battery was on the right; the convertible models had a similar boot lay-out.

The two-seaters had their batteries on the chassis below the tonneau area, accessible through a hinged trapdoor in the tonneau floor behind the seats. This trapdoor and its surround were colour-coded to match the trim and upholstery, except on cars with yellow trim where they were black. The spare wheel was positioned above the floor of the tonneau on two-seaters, half in the boot, half in the cockpit, and central in the car. The part of the spare wheel protruding into the cockpit was covered by a carpet or leathercloth bag, in various colour combinations to match the interior. The tool kit was stored in a roll, the kit being gradually reduced over the years. The roll was left loose in the boot, as was originally the jack, but this was later strapped down to the left-hand rear chassis extension or bumper bracket. A starting handle was not supplied.

A tonneau cover was supplied as standard on all early cars, with the exception of the so-called 'basic' 3000 Mark I. The two-seater tonneau cover was very straightforward, but the four-seater tonneau cover had a transverse support rail to be fitted in the hood sockets, and five longitudinal stiffeners in the rear part of the tonneau cover over the rear seats. Tonneau cover material and colours matched the hoods. The sidescreens supplied with these early cars had aluminium frames and sliding perspex windows. On the early BN4 models, only the front section of the window could be opened, but from chassis 47703 in September 1957 either the front or the rear half could be opened. The sidescreen had a pin fitting into a socket on the top of the door at the front, and the rear sidescreen bracket fitted on to a pin on a triangular chrome-plated backing plate on the inside door casing. Both front and rear brackets were secured by wingnuts.

The two-seater has this very simple 'one-and-a-half' bow hoodframe, always painted light grey, with two chrome-plated catches locking on to brackets on the windscreen pillars.

In this detail (right) the hood socket (behind) and the hard top mounting point (in front) can be clearly seen, along with the turnbuckle fastener and the first 'lift-the-dot' fastener for the hood cover.

This is the hood when stowed – it would normally be pushed further back, as far as it will go under the tonneau panel (right).

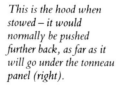

Still looking at the 3000 Mark I two-seater, this is the stirrup and the recess where the hoodframe rests when stowed (above).

The hood found on the Mark II and Mark III Convertible models was considered a great improvement, as it could be raised single-handedly from inside the car. A pull handle was fitted to the front hood rail for this purpose. The front and side rails were in one piece, back to about the rear edge of the side windows. At the front, the hood was secured to the windscreen pillars with hooks released by toggle catches. The hood frame had three bows and was rather more complex in design than on the earlier cars. The frame and the hood cover were permanently attached to the bodywork of the car. The rear window panel, however, could be folded down when the hood was raised. Originally this panel was attached to the main hood by two toggle catches but from body number 59372 (on late Mark II Convertibles, and on all Mark IIIs) the rear window panel was held in by a zip fastener. A hood cover was supplied with all cars, with a stowage bag.

The early type of sidescreen (above) on the 100-Six BN4 can instantly be recognised by the centre line sloping forward. This car should have windscreen pillars painted body colour, and demister slots painted to match the trim.

This is where the hood stows away on the four-seater, in a box behind the backrest of the rear seats (right). Note how the filler pieces at the top and sides are integral with the backrest.

The four-seater hoodframe is more complicated than a two-seater's, with three bows across the hood (right). This is the original type of 100-Six hoodframe, later modified. This frame should also be painted light grey.

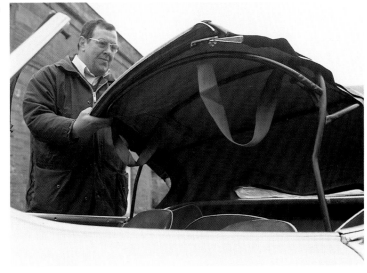

The early sidescreens were soon replaced by this type (above), with a rearwards sloping centre line, used on all subsequent 100-Six and 3000 models until the advent of the Convertible made sidescreens redundant.

The Convertible hood was a great improvement at the price of complexity This Mark II (BJ7) has the correct colour hood (blue on a blue and white car) but, according to our experts, some of the detailing is incorrect – such as the guttering round the side window, the rear window and the little 'ear behind the door.

Partly folded (or unfolded), the Convertible hood displays its complex frame (above), including the large integral front and side members. As on the earlier cars, the hoodframe should correctly be painted light grey.

This is about as far as the hood will collapse on a convertible (above right). When folded, the hood sits in this recess around the rear cockpit, rather than in a hidden hoodbox. Note the central grab handle on the front cross member of the hoodframe.

To cover the rather voluminous collapsed hood sitting on top of the car, the Convertibles wer supplied with this hoodba as standard (left).

Most of the 100-Six and 3000 two- and four-seater cars were supplied with a tonneau cover as standard, with exceptions as described in the text. This is the four-seater tonneau cover (above), fitted over the transverse support rail, but lacking the longitudinal stiffeners which should be fitted in the rear part of the tonneau cover behind the support rail.

The two-seater tonneau cover is simpler but still has a transverse support rail (right).

On the Convertible, the tonneau cover became an optional extra (right). Again there should be a transverse support rail – missing on this car. The small flaps on each side about halfway back are to allow the seat belts to pass through when the tonneau cover is used only to cover the rear seats, with the front portion stowed behind the front seats.

The tonneau cover was an extra on Convertibles, and while early Mark II Convertibles were only fitted with tonneau cover studs if a tonneau cover was to be supplied, these were installed on all cars from chassis 20392. As on earlier four-seater cars, a transverse tonneau cover support rail had to be fitted behind the seats. When the tonneau cover was used to cover only the rear seats, it was secured by fasteners to the heelboard. Bags were provided for stowing the tonneau cover and the two-piece support rail.

DASHBOARD AND INSTRUMENTS

The major change which occurred to the facia during the production run of the six-cylinder models was that a completely new facia was found on the 3000 Mark III, while all the previous models were similar.

The style and shape of the facia of the early cars was very similar to the original 100 model. The important differences introduced with the first 100-Six were that the facia panel and the top of the scuttle above it were covered in Vynide leathercloth to match the upholstery colour; a heater control panel was set into the lower edge of the facia centrally in the car; and the aperture for the steering column was now a hole through the panel, rather than a cut-out from the lower edge.

The instruments and some of the controls were set in front of the driver in a raised oval panel, surrounded by chrome-plated beading. On a right-hand drive car the rev counter was on the left and the speedometer on the right. These two instruments were transposed on left-hand drive cars, otherwise the lay-out was the same. The instrument dials had the reverse colour scheme of the 100: the two main instruments had flat black centres and silver-grey dished peripheries, and the two small instruments had silver-grey dials. Figures and lettering were black on the silver-grey background, with white lettering on the black centres of the main instruments. The pointers were black, with large chrome-plated centres on the main dials. The instruments were made by Smiths.

On the left of the instrument panel was the combined oil pressure gauge (above) and water temperature gauge (below). The oil pressure read to 100lb sq in, the thermometer to 230°F. A Celsius or Centigrade instrument was offered on some export cars on the 3000 Mark II from chassis 14240 in June 1961, reading to 110°C. Next followed the starter push-button marked 'S' in a round chrome-plated bezel, and below this was the wiper knob marked 'Wiper' in a hexagonal bezel. Below the edge of the facia at this point was the small switch for the panel lights.

The next instrument, continuing from left to right, was the rev counter (or, on left-hand drive cars, the speedometer). The rev counter read to 6000rpm in 1000rpm intervals but was red-lined at 4600rpm for the early BN4, at 4800rpm on 100-Six cars fitted with the six-port engine, and at 5200rpm on the 3000 models. At the bottom of the rev counter was a red ignition warning lamp. Immediately above the steering column aperture was a green direction indicator warning lamp in a round bezel. On the other side of the column was the speedometer (or, on a left-hand drive car, the rev counter). The speedometer read to 120mph (or 200kph) in intervals of 20. It had a three-figure and decimal trip recorder above, and a five-figure total mileage recorder below. The trip re-set button was below and behind the facia. At the bottom of the speedometer was a high beam warning lamp, originally red but changed to blue on some export cars from chassis 14171 on the 3000 Mark II.

To the right of the speedometer was the light switch in a hexagonal bezel, marked 'Side' and 'Head'. It pulled out to switch on the sidelamps and then turned to switch on the headlamps. On cars fitted with overdrive, the overdrive switch was below the light switch. This was a flick switch with a hexagonal bezel, and a round escutcheon plate marked 'Overdrive' in red letters above, 'Normal' in white letters below. Finally came the fuel gauge, marked in quarter intervals. The instruments all had chrome-plated bezels and rim lighting. The various knobs and switches were black with white lettering.

The heater control panel had three controls: the cold air pull on the left controlling the cold air intake shutter in the footwell, a slide in the middle controlling the temperature (or rather, the water inlet tap on the heater matrix), and a heater air volume control on the right (pull out to close). The knob on the temperature slide could be pulled out to switch on the blower. Above the heater controls on the main panel, to the left was found the windscreen washer push, and to the right the ignition lock in a hexagonal bezel. The ignition (and boot key) was usually an FP-series key, or

The facia and instuments (left) are similar on the six-cylinder models from the 100-Six (seen here) through the 3000 Mark I and Mark II, including the Mark II Convertible (BJ7) model. This illustration shows the unique bonnet with the centre crease, found only on some 100-Six models. A small point to watch: the two pairs of wires forming each spoke of the steering wheel are slightly further apart at the rim end than would be the case on a four-cylinder car. Another point is that the choke control on this car is under the facia rather than on the panel.

This detail shot (left) highlights the style of instruments common to all the six-cylinder cars from BN4 to BJ7 inclusive. On this 3000, the hornpush just has the figure '6' – a 100-Six would also have the figures '100' on the lightning flash.

This can be identified as a Mark II (left), and a late one at that, because it is fitted with the centre-change gearbox as opposed to the earlier cars with their off-set gearlevers. Black trim on a red car is in fact not correct on a Mark II. The demister slots should be painted to match the trim colour. The position of the radio control module under the parcel shelf is fairly typical of the early six-cylinder models before the Mark III Convertible.

The Mark III had a totally different facia, with wood veneer panels to either side, the Vynide-covered centre linking up with a console over the gearbox and propshaft tunnel (below). The glovebox compensated to some extent for the loss of the parcel shelf and door pockets. For the first time the radio and loudspeaker could be built in. The instruments were also completely revised (left) and now had all black dials rather than the previous two-tone dials.

This is the original type of washer bottle on the 100-Six (above, top), sitting in its hole in the parcel shelf. The washer control is on the facia panel above and to the left of the heater control panel. Note also the grabhandle and its dished backing plate, both chrome-plated.

On this 3000 Mark I, the washer bottle is the later type, and has moved its position in the parcel shelf (above, bottom). The choke control on the panel above the heater controls shows that this is a fairly late Mark I. The gearlever should be longer, with a cranked top, and the knob is not original.

on later Mark II cars an FS-series key, and the key number was stamped on the front of the lock barrel. The washer push and ignition lock were transposed on left-hand drive cars.

On the 100-Six cars and on the early 3000 Mark I, the choke pull was hidden away by the heater under the facia. Then for a short while in 1959, an automatic choke was fitted (compare the section on the fuel system and the 'Production Changes'); when the manual choke was re-introduced, the choke control was moved to the facia above the heater controls. On the passenger side of the facia was a chrome-plated grab

handle on an oval backing plate with a finger recess.

An Eversure rear view mirror with a chrome-plated back and stem was fitted on the scuttle; it had a ball fitting for adjustment. The two windscreen demister outlets were painted to match the colour of the facia and scuttle covering. If a radio was fitted on these early cars, the control module and loudspeaker were fixed on brackets under the facia.

On the 3000 Mark III Convertible (BJ8 model) the facia was totally changed. There were now wood veneer panels in front of the driver and passenger, usually with a grain pattern symmetrical around the centre line of the car. The centre panel of the facia was covered in Vynide to match the trim colour and was extended downwards to link up with the console over the propshaft tunnel. In front of the passenger was a glovebox with a lockable lid (the parcel shelf was discontinued). The veneer panels had chrome-plated finishers to their lower edges. The lay-out of the instruments and switches were complete mirror images on left-hand and right-hand drive cars, and the following description starts from the left on a left-hand drive car.

The first instrument was the fuel gauge, now a different type with a cut-out in the outer dial revealing an inner dial marked E, ½ and F. Next followed the oil pressure gauge and water temperature gauge. The speedometer was now marked to 140mph in 10mph intervals (or 240kph in 20kph intervals). The rev counter was now the electronic type rather than driven mechanically, and read up to 7000rpm in 500rpm intervals. Above 5000rpm was a narrow orange zone and a wide red zone indicating the recommended rev limit. All of the instruments now had all-black dials with white figures, letters and pointers. Between the rev counter and the speedometer were two green arrow direction indicator warning lights, above the steering column slot. On the side of the instrument panel towards the centre were the choke pull and the windscreen washer push.

On the centre panel itself were the heater controls at the top. Below these was a chrome-plated panel with a row of four black toggle switches, two and two either side of the central ignition lock. From the left on a left-hand drive car (or from the right on a right-hand drive car) these switches operated the overdrive (down to engage), the wipers, the panel lights and the lights (two steps down, for sidelamps and headlamps respectively). If overdrive was not fitted, a switch for auxiliary equipment was installed. The functions of the switches were marked in white letters on the panel above them. The ignition lock no longer had the key number stamped on it, but it was an FS series key which also operated the other locks on the car. The ignition key also operated the starter. If a 3000 was fitted with the combined ignition and steering lock, the holes for the ignition lock (and on earlier cars, the starter button) were covered by blanking plates.

Below the switch panel was a built-in loudspeaker grille, and below this was a space for the radio control module. If a radio was not fitted this was covered by a plate bearing the 3000 lightning flash also found on the boot lid. The scuttle was covered in Vynide as on earlier cars but now always black, with a centrally placed mirror and demister outlets as before. If no specific mention has been made of a change in the description of the Mark III facia, it may be assumed that it followed the detailing of the earlier cars.

EXPORT VARIATIONS

For the original 100 model, export variations had not really been necessary, other than in the most basic terms – such as left-hand drive or right-hand drive steering, miles-per-hour or kilometres-per-hour speedometer, provision of different headlamps, and the deletion of the heater on cars for hot climates (Australia). However, as the fifties wore on and turned into the sixties, it became necessary to provide more and more variations to cope with changing legal requirements in different export markets.

In August 1958, possibly from car number BN6-L/2878, cars for export to Germany (and Switzerland) were fitted with octagonal hub nuts rather than knock-ons, where wire wheels were specified. Such cars were supplied with a special spanner in the tool kit. From 1966 onwards, these octagonal nuts were also fitted to some cars for the USA.

Throughout the production run there were the usual variations in headlamp types for different markets. Originally, cars for North America may have been supplied with empty headlamp shells for local installation of sealed beam units, but the sealed beam headlamps were definitely fitted at the factory from July 1959 onwards

(BT7/2194, BN7/2276). A little later (chassis number 9239, April 1960) cars for Sweden were fitted with the then-new assymmetrical dip headlamps, which were probably also fitted to other European export cars later on.

At the rear of the car, reflectors were changed to conform with new US legislation in 1960, and in December of that year they were relocated to bumper-mounted brackets on some export cars. Separate front and rear indicators with amber lenses were found on cars for Germany and Sweden as early as chassis 15163 in September 1961. Twin numberplate lamps were fitted on European export cars from body 78042 in September 1965, and were found on German cars rather earlier than this. It should also be mentioned that the numberplate backing plates found on home market cars were usually replaced by simple brackets on export cars, adjustable to suit a variety of numberplate shapes and sizes.

In mechanical terms, the most important variation happened in October 1962 when French export cars were fitted with the under-bored 2860cc engines to suit French vehicle excise duty, which is based on the CV formula (indirectly depending on cubic capacity). This penalizes cars of more than 15CV (approximately 2.9-litres) quite severely. These engines were identified by their 29FF and 29KF prefixes and also featured special ignition suppression equipment to minimize radio broadcasting interference. Some cars for France were later fitted with 2912cc engines nevertheless, with prefix 29KFA.

While the standard fan always had four blades, fans with six, eight and even 16 blades were available for export markets at different times. From chassis 13601 in January 1961, some European export cars had the so-called 'Continental' exhaust system which featured a second silencer transversely mounted at the back of the car, with the tailpipe on the right-hand side. However, this was discontinued when the Mark III model was introduced with its more efficient exhaust system.

Inside, a Centigrade thermometer became available as an alternative to the Fahrenheit instrument from chassis 14240 in June 1961, and was always fitted from then on to cars with kilometres speedometers. From chassis 15163 in September 1961, cars for Germany and Sweden became fitted with a combined steering and ignition lock, also

incorporating a key-operated starter. On such cars the ignition lock and starter button were deleted from the facia.

Other little local peccadilloes resulted in cars for Canada being fitted with towing eyes from chassis 20880 in September 1962. Canadian cars also at times had special heavy-duty batteries fitted locally, being shipped without batteries. In June 1967, from chassis 41930, cars for France and the Benelux countries were fitted with a transparent brake fluid reservoir. This necessitated the brake and clutch fluids, which otherwise shared one reservoir, having two separate reservoirs. Also around this time, possibly from body number 86904 (chassis number 42039) in July 1967, some cars for the USA were fitted with special high impact resistant windscreens (all windscreens were always from laminated glass).

The heater was not standard equipment on either the 100-Six or the 3000, and was usually not fitted to export cars to hot climates, on which the thermostat might also be deleted. I have found one reference to a headlamp flasher switch being offered as an optional extra on the 3000 Mark III, primarily I suppose for export (again to Germany) but I have never come across a car so equipped.

Both whitewall tyres and Dunlop SP.41 radial tyres were on the list of optional equipment, but it is a reasonable assumption that whitewall tyres were predominantly found on cars for the USA, and radial tyres mainly on cars for France (and possibly other European countries). It may also be mentioned that Mark III cars for the USA almost without exception were fitted with the following extras as standard: wire wheels, overdrive, heater and adjustable steering column. In the USA, radios were normally dealer-installed rather than factory-fitted. The optional leather upholstery (for the Mark III) was not offered in the USA.

There was some cross-breeding among different export models. One good example is that many cars built to German or French specification were fitted with miles-per-hour speedometers, as they were ordered by American servicemen in Europe (and often as not in due course found their way across the Atlantic). Another was the right-hand drive cars supplied to a few die-hard Swiss customers even in the sixties – they were considered preferable for Alpine motoring, as you could more easily keep an eye on the kerb!

Production Changes

In this summary, the different numbers are indicated as follows: C = car or chassis number; C/E = unified car (chassis)/engine number; E = engine number; B = body number. Car/chassis and engine number prefixes have been used to indicate different models as required.

100-Six Models

BN4-L/22598   May 56
First Longbridge-built car (first RHD car was BN4/22880 in June 1956. Series production from August 1956.

C.35707 LHD   Feb 57
C.35827 RHD
Longer front coil springs, raising front end of car, to improve appearance and ride characteristics.

E.40501   Apr 57
Fully-floating gudgeon pins to pistons.

C.41124 RHD   May 57
C.41135 LHD
RH seat and carpet modified to improve clearance between handbrake and propshaft tunnel.

C.47184 RHD   Aug 57
C.47191 LHD
Air deflectors added on each side, between radiator and radiator grille.

C.47703 LHD   Sep 57
C.47865 RHD
Revised sidescreens, rear half of perspex now sliding instead of fixed.

C.48114 RHD   Sep 57
C.48387 LHD
Left-hand external door handle with lock replaced by non-locking plain type.

E.48863 (some cars)   Oct 57
E.52602 (all cars)   Nov 57
Introduction of six-port engine. New cylinder head, inlet manifold separate. Larger 1¾in HD6 carburettors. Bigger valves. Higher compression ratio. Solid-skirt pistons. Various attendant changes. Also at C.48863, clutch and brake master cylinders with integral reservoirs replaced, new remote combined clutch and brake reservoir introduced.

C/E.50759   Nov 57
First Abingdon-built car. Snap-lock instead of spring-loaded ball joints to accelerator control rod linkage.

C.52704   Dec 57
B.7320
Bulkhead panel strengthened around gearbox aperture, to reduce scuttle shake at high speed.

C/E.54285   Dec 57
Highest known number for a Longbridge-built car.

C.54755   Jan 58
Windscreen assembly improved to prevent glass breakage.

C.60413   Mar 58
HP-type fuel pump replaced by high-capacity LCS-type.

C/E.62190   Apr 58
Highest number in first batch of Abingdon-built BN4.

C.BN6/501   Mar 58
First BN6 car.

C.BN6/1183   May 58
Trafalgar windscreen washer (glass bottle) replaced by Tudor (plastic bottle).

C.BN6/1995   Jul 58
New high-efficiency steering gear, ratio changed from 14:1 to 15:1.

C.BN6/2030   Jul 58
Radiator thermometer pick-up moved from header tank to thermostat housing.

C.BN6/2878   Aug 58
Modified clutch slave cylinder. Octagonal hub nuts on cars with wire wheels for Germany and Switzerland.

C.BN4/68960★   Sep 58
First car in second batch of Abingdon-built BN4. Incorporating BN6 modifications as detailed above. Adjustable steering column now optional rather than standard. New hood frame. Bonnet prop moved from left-hand to right-hand. Door Furflex seals now colour-coded, but all boot mats now black. Also other smaller modifications. ★68960 was the first car in this batch but 16 cars built after this had lower C/E. numbers from 67273 upwards.

C.BN4/70165   Sep 58
C.BN6/3395
Non-adjustable steering column lengthened by ½in for better clearance to facia.

C.BN4/72850   Oct 58
Battery fixing rod lengthened by 5⁄16in (BN4 model only).

C.BN6/4022   Nov 58
Front apron panel added (BN6 model only).

C.BN4/74421   Dec 58
C.BN6/4319
Locating ring added to petrol filler pipe, to prevent air locks.

C.BN4/77766   Mar 59
C.BN6/4650
100-Six models discontinued.

3000 models

C.101   Mar 59
(E.29D/101)
3000 model introduced. Main modifications from 100-Six: engine bored out to 2912cc. Cylinders siamesed in pairs. Compression ratio 9.0:1. 10in clutch. Stronger gears, revised gear and overdrive ratios. Disc brakes on front wheels.

E.29D/663   Apr 59
White metal bearings replaced by lead-indium type.

E.29D/895   Apr 59
Hobourn-Eaton rotary vane type oil pump replaced by gear pump.

E.29D/2772   Jun 59
Champion N.5 plugs introduced as alternative to N.3.

C.2194   Jul 59
E.29D/2864
Thermo-electric choke instead of manual. Choke control discontinued.

C.BT7/2194   Jul 59
C.BN7/2276
Cars for North America now fitted with sealed beam headlamps at the factory.

E.29D/3079   Jul 59
68°C/154°F thermostat instead of 70°C/158°F.

C.BN7/5234   Nov 59
C.BT7/5310
Thermo-electric choke deleted, manual choke re-introduced. Choke control now on main facia panel. (This change occurred from E.29D/6369 intermittently, 29D/6395 all.)

C.BT7/6320   Dec 59
C.BN7/6487
New radiator for improved cooling, 12 gills per inch instead of 10 gills per inch.

C.BT7/6345   Dec 59
C.BT7/6487
Windscreen washer bottle with larger filler neck.

E.29D/10544   Feb 60
Improved gearbox mainshaft assembly.

E.10897 o/d   Feb 60
E.11342 std   Mar 60
More rigid gears introduced. Plain bushes instead of needle roller bearings to layshaft. Gear ratios revised.

C.8222   Feb 60
Improved design of battery fixing rods.

C.BT7/9088 Mar/Apr 60
C.BN7/9450
Dust covers fitted to front disc brakes. Car/chassis numbers indicate first disc wheel cars so fitted; first wire wheel cars were C.BT7/9090 and C.BN7/9453.

C.9239 Apr 60
Cars for Sweden fitted with assymmetrical dip headlamps.

C.BT7/9389 May 60
C.BN7/9453
Rear reflectors on cars for USA changed to conform with new US legislation.

E.14566 o/d Jun 60
E.14910 std
Needle roller bearings re-introduced for gearbox layshaft.

C.BT7/10299 Jun 60
C.BN7/10309
Road Speed tyres RS5 fitted instead of RS4.

C.BT7/10303 Jun 60
C.BN7/10329
Revised front coil spring rates for improved road holding.

C.BN7/10842 Jun 60
C.BT7/10876
Rubber sleeve cover fitted to fuel pump.

E.29D/18656 Jul 60
Improved fast idle mechanism for carburettors.

E.29D/20598 Aug 60
Gearlever cranked at top to improve gear change.

C.13488 Dec 60
Some export cars fitted with joint bracket for rear numberplate and lamp. Also for export, rear reflectors relocated on brackets to bumper.

C.13531 Dec 60
Revised design of rear numberplate lamp with two bulbs.

C.13601 Jan 61
Six-blade fan optional on export cars. Cars for Europe fitted with 'Continental exhaust system' incorporating a second transverse silencer at the back of the car with the tailpipe on the right-hand side.

C.13751 Mar 61
(E.29E/101)
Introduction of Mark II model. Now fitted three HS4 carburettors. New camshaft. Vibration damper added to timing chain. Various attendant changes. Seat belt mounting points built into body structure. Vertical bar radiator grille.

C.13831 Mar 61
Fuel pump specifications upgraded from AUA72 to AUA172.

C.14171 May 61
Main beam warning light colour changed from red to blue on export cars with kilometres speedometers.

C.14240 Jun 61
Centigrade thermometer optional on export cars. From now on, always found on cars with kilometres speedometers.

C.14378 Jun 61
Accelerator relay shaft and lever welded rather than bolted.

E.29E/929 Jun 61
Carburettor balance pipe increased in diameter. Improved, single-piece asbestos insulation both sides of carburettor heat shield.

C.14922 Aug 61
Improved material specification for valve springs.

C.15104 Aug 61
Brake servo optional extra, brakes on cars thus equipped modified to suit. More robust accelerator pedal shaft lever, pedal modified to suit.

C.15163 Sep 61
Cars for Germany and Sweden fitted with combined steering and ignition lock, key-operated starter (two alternative types of lock). These cars also fitted with separate amber lens direction indicators front and rear; body modified to suit.

E.29E/2246 Nov 61
C.BT7/15881
C.BN7/16039
New gearbox, with top selectors and centre change (as opposed to side change). Ratios unchanged. Fibreglass gearbox cover. Various attendant changes to body and trim. Shorter speedometer cable. New brake and clutch pedal levers. Also at E.29F/2246, new water pump, one-piece spindle/bearing with interference fit fan belt pulley.

E.29E/2995 Nov 61
Carburettor floats of nylon instead of metal.

C.BT7/17129 Jan 62
C.BN7/17236
Revised setting for front shock absorbers.

C.BT7/17352 Jan 62
C.BN7/17547
Fuel pump moved from left-hand to right-hand side of car to avoid vaporisation due to exhaust heat. Fuel pump specification now AUA173.

C.BJ7/17551 Jan 62
B.55000
E.29F/101
First Convertible model. Two HS6 carburettors. Body revised with wrap-around windscreen, new hood, doors with quarterlights and wind-down windows. Coil spring rates revised.

C.18764 Mar 62
New headlamps for North American cars.

C.BN7/18888 Mar 62
Two-seater model discontinued.

C.19191 Apr 62
Non-lubricated nylon-seated ball joints for steering connections.

C.BT7/19853 Jun 62
Four-seater model discontinued.

C.BJ7/20110 Jun 62
One-piece rubber seal for quarterlights.

C.BJ7/20126 Jun 62
Windscreen washer tubing increased from $\frac{3}{16}$ to $\frac{1}{4}$in diameter, new control module with single outlet and revised tubing layout.

C.BJ7/20392 Aug 62
Tonneau cover studs fitted as standard to all cars.

C.BJ7/20880 Sep 62
Towing eyes added to cars for Canada only.

E.29F/2012 Sep 62
New crankshaft main bearings.

E.29F/2269 Sep 62
New type of Tecalemit oil filter (Purolator not changed).

E.29F/2286 Sep 62
New camshaft and outer valve springs.

E.29FF/101 Oct 62
(C.BJ7/21049)
2860cc engine fitted to export cars for France. These engines also fitted with special ignition suppression equipment, including special h/t leads, plug caps and shielding for distributor.

E.29F/2592 Dec 62
Bellows thermostat replaced by wax type (83°C/182°F).

E.29F/2724 Jan 63
Champion UN12Y plugs instead of N.5.

E.29F/3563 Feb 63
C.BJ7/22695
Distributor with pre-tilted contact beakers introduced; type 25D6 instead of type DM6A.

B.59372 Apr 63
Zip fastener in place of toggle catches for hood rear window.

E.29F/4898 May 63
9½in diaphragm spring clutch introduced.

C.BJ7/24367 Jun 63
48-spoke wire wheels replaced by 60-spoke wheels.

B.60792 Aug 63
New wiper motor, type DR3A instead of DR2.

C.BJ8/25315
B.70200
E.29K/101
(29KF/101) Oct 63
Mark III model introduced. New camshaft and valve springs. HD8 2in carburettors. New dual exhaust system with extra silencers at rear, right-hand tail pipe. Servo brakes standard. New wood facia. Centre console fitted. Key-operated starter. New fusebox, control box and dynamo. New mainshaft to gearbox, gear ratios revised. Windscreen washer bottle with larger neck fitted under bonnet. Ambla trim fitted as standard, revised seat pattern. Hinged rear seat squab converts to luggage platform. Electronic rev counter, 140mph speedometer. New switchgear.

C.BJ8/25400 Nov 63
Detail change to brake servo unit air filter.

E.29K/279 Nov 63
Longer dipstick positioned higher up on cylinder block.

C.BJ8/26705 May 64
'Phase II' model. Chassis members re-profiled under rear axle. Six-leaf rear springs. Panhard rod deleted. Radius arms to rear axle, fitted on pedestals topped with rubber bumpers. Net result improved ground clearance at rear. Rear shock absorber arms modified to suit. Front sidelamps/indicators with larger lenses. Modified disc brakes. Wire wheel hubs with coarser threads (8 t.p.i.). New handed front swivel axle assemblies. Push-button door handles with external locks on both sides. Longer arm rest to propshaft tunnel in place of short, hinged arm rest with cubbyhole. Detail changes to interior trim. Some export cars with one-piece fans, eight and later 16 fan blades.

C.BJ8/28225 Aug 64
Fuel pump specification upgraded to AUF301.

E.29K/4108 Oct 64
9in instead of 9½in clutch.

B.76138 Mar 65
C.BJ8/31336 (approx)
All cars now fitted with separate amber front/rear indicators, and rear reflectors on brackets to bumper.

C.BJ8/31931 May 65
Horns modified.

B.78042 Sep 65
Two numberplate lamps on European export cars (found on cars for Germany from B.75208). Headlamps type Mark X instead of Mark VI.

B.78154 Oct 65
Changed material specification for red colour carpet only.

B.79900 Feb 66
Modified numberplate bracket on North American cars.

E.29K/10272 Mar 66
Crankshaft pulley with built-in damper. V-section fan belt, other pulleys modified to suit.

B.81366 May 66
Headlamps modified.

B.82776 Aug 66
Shape of liner to rear quarter modified, corner of wheel arch/floor cut away.

C.BJ8/41930 Jun 67
Transparent brake fluid reservoir fitted to cars for export to Benelux and France (these cars fitted with separate clutch fluid reservoir).

C.BJ8/42039 Jul 67
B.86904
High-impact windscreen fitted to some cars for USA.

C.BJ8/43026 Mar 68
Last car manufactured (series production had been discontinued in Nov/Dec 67 with C.BJ8/43025).

OPTIONS, EXTRAS AND ACCESSORIES

The 100-Six was not in absolute terms as well equipped as the 100 had been. But that at least kept the list price down! According to one brochure, there were two models: the 'standard' with disc wheels and tubeless tyres, single-tone paintwork and lacking overdrive; and the 'de-luxe' with overdrive, two-tone paintwork, wire wheels and Road Speed tyres. Road Speed tyres were in fact fitted if either wire wheels, or an overdrive, or both, were specified; the tubeless tyres were only found on disc wheel cars without overdrive.

However, wire wheels, Road Speed tyres, overdrive and two-tone paintwork could all be ordered individually. The heater was technically an extra – it cost extra – and was sometimes not found on home market cars (apart from some export models). A hard top (compare list of colour schemes) and a factory-fitted radio (usually a Radiomobile) were offered as extras. The tonneau cover was standard. An adjustable steering column was standard on the early BN4 cars, but was an option on the BN6 and the BN4 from chassis 68960 onwards.

On the original 3000 models, the list of factory-fitted extras was more or less as for the 100-Six, except that Road Speed tyres were now fitted as standard and the tonneau cover was deleted from the 'basic' model (which also lacked overdrive and was fitted with disc wheels). A new addition to the list of extras were Ace Mercury wheeldiscs (for the disc wheels) which persisted in the parts list right up to the end of the Mark III model although I have never come across a car fitted with them – they were quite horrible! Wing mirrors (one or two) became available, originally either round or the trapezoidal-shape 'boomerang' type. An external luggage rack could be fitted, and if this was supplied factory-fitted a wing mirror on the driver's side was also always added. The luggage rack and wing mirrors may also have been available for the 100-Six models. A cigar lighter and a locking petrol filler cap were offered on the 3000 models from the start.

The Mark II model was offered with the same options as the Mark I, with the important addition of a brake servo, optional from chassis number 15104 in 1961. When the convertible model (BJ7) came out in 1962, the tonneau cover was discontinued as standard equipment and was now an extra, and the hard top disappeared altogether. Fog and/or spot

This is the correct style of factory hard top offered for the 100-Six and 3000 two- and four-seater models, here painted Ivory White but also available in other colours. The wrap-around rear window with the two supports inside is a particularly distinctive feature.

lamps were now listed as extras, and may have been offered on earlier cars. Only the boomerang type of wing mirror was quoted for the BJ7 (and BJ8) models. Whitewall tyres or Dunlop SP41 radial tyres were now offered as alternatives to the standard Road Speed tyres (and may also have been available previously).

As the Mark III model (BJ8) was fitted with Ambla upholstery as standard, leather (or hide) upholstery became available as an extra. On the other hand, the BJ8 had the brake servo fitted as standard. Not all factory-fitted extras were offered in the American market (for instance, leather upholstery) but similar extras were then usually made available by the importers or as dealer fitments. For instance US-sold cars had locally-fitted radios instead of the factory-fitted Radiomobile unit. Otherwise, the list of extras for the Mark III was much as before, and it is important to realise that right up until the end of production it was possible to order a BJ8 on disc wheels, without overdrive, and without the heater.

Later brochures quoted a luggage rack, a badge bar, wing mirror(s), fog and driving lamps (with extra switch panel) and seat belts as being available for dealer fitment. All these were part of the growing range of accessories offered by BMC Service Limited. They also offered rubber over-mats and seat covers (even in mock leopard skin!) to suit the 3000. The seat belts could be fitted to any car from the start of Mark II production (chassis 13751 in 1961) without modification, and to earlier 100-Six and 3000 cars if mounting points were installed (a modification kit was made available). The recommended seat belts were Kangol Magnet three-point type, usually supplied under the BMC Service label.

No special tuning modifications appear to have been made generally available for the 100-Six or 3000 models, although the works rally and race cars often differed considerably from standard specification. Some even had three Weber carburettors apart from other interesting modifications. But this is strictly speaking irrelevant as far as the original specification of the standard cars is concerned, and so is any modification by outside engine tuners.

However, although documentation is hard to come by, I understand that Healey at Warwick offered a four-wheel Dunlop disc brake conversion kit for the 100-Six, and possibly also a louvred bonnet. Shades of the 100M and 100S! Rear disc brakes were offered for the 3000. If any such modification can be proved to be the contemporary work of Healeys, it would certainly add to the interest of a car so equipped.

IDENTIFICATION, DATING AND PRODUCTION FIGURES

When the first 100-Six was introduced in 1956, Austin at Longbridge was still using the unified car/engine number system which meant that the same number was used for chassis number and engine number (please compare the earlier section for the Austin-Healey 100). Also, the 100-Six series of numbers was shared with other models, in this case the various Westminster saloons (A90, A105 and A95). A few pre-production cars were built from May to August 1956, with series production commencing in August. The first chassis/engine number quoted for a BN4 model was 22598.

The car/chassis number prefix was BN4. Note still the letter N for two-seater body although the car was now an 'occasional four-seater', 4 denoted the fourth series of Austin-Healey (prefixes BN3 and later BN5 were found on one-off prototype cars). A left-hand drive car had the prefix BN4-L. These prefixes were usually followed by an S on cars not fitted with overdrive (S for either Standard or Synchromesh), or by the letter O on cars fitted with Overdrive. Originally the engine prefix was 1C-H, denoting first type of C-series engine, the H indicating probably High compression (or, possibly, Healey specification). However, the engine prefix was later changed, possibly coinciding with the introduction of the six-port engine in 1957. These engines had the prefix 26D, followed by U on non-overdrive cars, and R (or RU) on overdrive cars, finishing with the letter H for High compression. If low compressions were found (which I doubt), they would have the letter L here.

BN4 body numbers started a new series from 1 upwards. The body numbers were still prefixed with four-figure body batch numbers but regrettably less is known about these batch numbers than is the case for the 100 body batch numbers. However most seem to be above 3000. The body numbers on Longbridge-built cars ran up to approximately 7100. Some early Abingdon-built cars had much lower body numbers, but generally speaking most

Abingdon-built cars had body numbers from 6878 and upwards. The first batch of Abingdon cars had body numbers to 8819, the second batch had body numbers from 9001 to 11301. The body number was found on the edge of the bonnet on all six-cylinder cars as it had been on the 100, but only the 100-Six had the body number stamped on the back of the cockpit trim strips.

Production at Longbridge continued until December 1957, the highest known chassis/engine number issued to a Longbridge car being 54285. The later Longbridge-built cars often had the six-port engine (see 'Production Changes'). Abingdon production got under way on a regular basis in November 1957, the lowest chassis/engine number on an Abingdon-built car being 50759. The Abingdon-built cars also had an additional 'allocation' number; these were issued from 501 upwards and are also known as 'serial' numbers. As indicated there were two batches of BN4 cars built at Abingdon. The first batch was made between November 1957 and April 1958. Then production was for a time switched completely to the BN6 model, and BN4 production was resumed in September 1958, continuing until March 1959.

The following details give the identifying car/engine and allocation (serial) numbers for the two Abingdon batches:

Batch 1: Car/engine numbers 50759 to 62190 (approx)
Allocation ·numbers 501 to 2441

Batch 2: Car/engine numbers 68960 (67273) (approx) to 77766
Allocation numbers 2442 to 4741

It is difficult to be too dogmatic about the car/engine numbers which were never issued in strict order. Therefore, the following list of first and last numbers in each year is also somewhat approximate:

1956: 22598 to approx 32000
1957: approx 32000 to approx 54500 (to allocation number 829?)
1958: approx 54500 to approx 74400 (allocation numbers 830 to 3623?)
1959: approx 74400 to 77766 (allocation numbers 3624 to 4741)

In fact, it is quite likely that the sequence of allocation numbers or the body number sequence gives a better picture of the order in which the cars were actually built.

The two–seater model of 1958 was given the chassis number prefix BN6 with an extra L on Left-hand drive cars. Following the Abingdon rather than the Longbridge principles, BN6 chassis numbers started with 501 and ran to 4650. This model shared the engine number series (and engine prefixes) with the BN4. BN6 cars had engine numbers from 60044 (or 60949?) up to 77765. The model had its own series of body numbers, starting from 2 and running up to 4151. The production period was from March 1958 to March 1959. Approximate first and last chassis numbers in each year were as follows:

1958: 501 to 4321
1959: 4322 to 4650

As far as is known, the Austin-Healey 100 had never been offered in CKD (Completely Knocked Down) kit form for assembly in selected export markets, but the 100-Six was available in this form. Little is known about Longbridge-sourced CKD cars, which are thought all to have been RHD cars destined for South Africa, and there may have been as many as 175 of them in 1956–57. Abingdon contributed mainly BN6 CKD cars: 85 RHD cars for South Africa, 23 LHD cars (of which five to Cuba, the rest to Mexico), and only a further three BN4 CKD cars which had LHD and went to Cuba. The Cuba-bound cars just preceded the Castro revolution – they were not totally knocked down and may more appropriately be called SKD or Semi-Knocked Down cars.

The Longbridge BN4 production figures are only available in the same form as the figures for the 100 model, and it is not possible to break them down in any more detail. They are as follows:

1956–57: 5541
1957–58: 1512 – for a total of 7053 cars

Abingdon's production control department could and did improve considerably on this, and they produced much more detailed figures, with the exception that originally they did not split LHD cars between North American and non-North American models (they only began to do so with the 3000 Mark II Convertible). I have therefore gone through the records for the earlier models and have produced these figures separately in table 1.

It will be noted from table 1 that the total production figures for the two models exactly match the series of allocation numbers (BN4) and chassis numbers

TABLE 1 Abingdon 100-Six production

BN4	RHD home	RHD export	LHD export	LHD NA export	CKD RHD	CKD LHD	Total
1957	14	0	26	289	0	0	329
1958	121	81	399	2190	0	3	2794
1959	21	6	110	981	0	0	1118
Total	156	87	535	3460	0	3	4241

BN6	RHD home	RHD export	LHD export	LHD NA export	CKD RHD	CKD LHD	Total
1958	118	40	324	3237	85	17	3821
1959	15	5	18	285	0	6	329
Total	133	45	342	3522	85	23	4150

The 100-Six BN4 used the same type of car/ engine number plate as the later 100 BN1 and BN2 models. On this Abingdon-built car, there is a supplementary plate underneath and below, quoting the 'serial number' (also known as the Abingdon allocation number) which indicates the build sequence of the Abingdon BN4s. The BN6 has a different type of car number plate. Note also the body number plate above the car number plate, with the batch number above on the left, the actual body number below on the right.

This 3000 Mark I has a chassis plate of the type which would also have been found on a 100-Six BN6, quoting only the car (chassis) number. On the body number plate the model code BN7 has been added. Later 3000 models had a chassis plate with rounded ends and space for the car number only.

TABLE 2 Identification of 3000 models

	Mark I 2-str	Mark I 4-str	Mark II 2-str	Mark II 4-str	Mark II Conv	Mark III Conv
Chassis no. prefix	H-BN7	H-BT7	H-BN7	H-BT7	H-BJ7	H-BJ8
Chassis nos. (from-to)	186-13734	101-13750	13991-18888	13751-19853	17551-25314	25315-43026
Production period (from-to)	Mar 59- May 61	Mar 59- May 61	May 61- Mar 62	May 61- Jun 62	May 62- Nov 63	Oct 63- Mar 68
Engine no. prefix	29D	29D	29E	29E	29F; 29FF★	29K; 29KF★
Engine nos. (from-to)	101-26212	101-26212	101-5799	101-5799	101-6188	101-17631
Body nos. (from-to)	701-(12763)	101-(13787)	(12764)-19129	(13788)-19239	55000-60999 70000-70166	70200-87903

★The 29FF and 29KF types of engines were the 2860cc engines fitted to export cars for France; engine number series were 29F/101-157, 29KF/101-399. Some later French engines were of 2912cc, type 29KFA, from engine number 29KFA/224.

(BN6). There do not appear to have been any chassis-only deliveries. The total number of BN4 models made, Longbridge and Abingdon together, was 11294 cars.

The 100-Six cars all had their car/chassis numbers stamped on a maker's guarantee plate found on the rear bulkhead of the engine compartment. The style of plate is slightly different depending on whether it is a BN4 or a BN6. Near the chassis number plate will also be found the body number plate. Abingdon-built BN4 cars also had a plate marked 'serial number' just below the chassis number plate, the 'serial number' being the 'allocation number' referred to above. The engine number was stamped on a small tag affixed to the left-hand side of the cylinder block at the front of the engine. The location and style of plates were carried forward to the 3000 models. Some German export cars had a different type of plate which also gave the maximum permitted front and rear axle loads, to comply with German (TüV) regulations.

With the introduction of the 3000 models in 1959, the chassis numbering system was brought into line with the proper BMC system then coming into use. First of all, the 3000 chassis number series commenced with the number 101. Secondly, the prefixes were given an extra letter to start with, indicating make of car, this being H for (Austin-)Healey. The third change was that the 'four-seater' model was now given the letter T indicating this body style, while the two-seater stuck with the letter N, and the later Convertible models were given the letter J. As ever, LHD cars were given an extra L in the prefix. However, towards the end of production, in approximately June 1967, North American specification cars were given the letter U instead of L in the prefix. Also on these later cars, the chassis numbers were suffixed with the letter G indicating that assembly had taken place in

TABLE 3 Dating 3000 models by chassis number

	BT7	BN7	BJ7	BJ8
1959	101- 6520	186-6686		
1960	6521-13561	6831-13538		
1961	13562-17126	13539-17051		
1962	17127-19853	17052-18888	17551-21782	
1963			21783-25314	25315-25658
1964				25659-30532
1965				30533-34479
1966				34480-39974
1967				39975-43025
1968				43026 only

NB: For the sake of simplicity, this table does not distinguish between the Mark I and Mark II models of the BT7 and BN7 cars. Last Mark I and first Mark II chassis numbers are quoted in table 2.

This style of engine number plate is found on all six-cylinder engines, on the left-hand side of the cylinder block towards the front. The prefix 29D reveals that we are looking at a 3000 Mark I.

TABLE 4 3000 production figures

Mark I BT7	RHD home	RHD export	LHD export	LHD NA export	CKD RHD	CKD LHD	Total
1959	212	54	301	4184	5	6	4762
1960	386	67	904	4517	30	16	5920
1961	74	9	19	31	10	0	143
Total	672	130	1224	8732	45	22	**10825**

Mark I BN7	RHD home	RHD export	LHD export	LHD NA export	CKD RHD	CKD LHD	Total
1959	68	22	168	1422	5	6	1691
1960	72	4	122	852	35	0	1085
1961	17	5	12	10	5	0	49
Total	157	31	302	2284	45	6	**2825**

Mark II BT7	RHD home	RHD export	LHD export	LHD NA export	CKD RHD	Chassis only LHD	Total
1961	171	30	518	2431	5	0	3155
1962	90	8	83	1759	0	1★	1941
Total	261	38	601	4190	5	1	**5096**

★This was chassis no. 19804 which ended up as the Pininfarina-built 'Firrere' fastback GT coupé – the only documented chassis-only delivery ever.

Mark II BN7	RHD home	RHD export	LHD export	LHD NA export	Total
1961	25	2	53	134	214
1962	9	3	4	125	141
Total	34	5	57	259	**355**

Mark II BJ7	RHD home	RHD export	LHD export	LHD NA export	Total
1962	126	15	277	2163	2581
1963	329	29	318	2856	3532
Total	455	44	595	5019	**6113**

the **MG** factory at Abingdon.

The 3000 engine numbers had prefixes commencing with 29 indicating the capacity of the engine. This was followed by one or two further letters indicating the type of engine. Next came one or two code letters indicating the type of transmission, either RU on overdrive cars, or just U on non-overdrive cars. Finally came the letter H for High compression (or L for Low compression if found). Engine number series started with 101 for each type of engine. The body numbers were still prefixed with the body batch number,

usually above 3000, but were now followed by the model identification code – BT7, BN7, BJ7 or BJ8, and sometimes with an L on LHD cars. The Mark I and Mark II models shared one series of body numbers, allocated in batches to two- or four-seater models, starting from 101. The Convertible models had a new series of body numbers. Table 2 gives further details of the number brackets found on the different models. Please note that *all* 3000 models shared the same series of car/chassis numbers, for the Mark I and II models allocated in batches depending body style.

Table 2 requires a few additional explanatory notes. The reason why Mark I engine numbers went as high as 26212 was that the series of engine numbers was shared with engines destined for the Austin A99 Westminster saloon (!). The split in the body number series quoted for the Mark I/II two- and four-seater models above is approximate – even arbitrary! Body numbers were never used in exact order. The first BJ7 convertible, 17551, was in fact built in January 1962, but series production only started in May. Only from 19854 were all cars convertibles. It is not known why

Mark III BJ8	RHD home	RHD export	LHD export	LHD NA export	Others†	Total
1963	0	0	1	343	0	344
1964, Phase I	(108)	(7)	(81)	(850)	0	(1046)
1964, Phase II	(314)	(23)	(287)	(3200)	(4)	(3828)
1964, total	422	30	368	4050	4	4874
1965	310	28	325	3281	3	3947
1966	237	19	238	5000	1	5495
1967	176	14	128	2733	0	3051
1968	1	0	0	0	0	1
Total, Phase I	108	7	82	1193	0	1390
Total, Phase II	1038	84	978	14214	8	16322
Total	1146	91	1060	15407	8	**17712**

†These eight cars had chassis numbers allocated but were not built on the normal production line, and were not originally counted by Abingdon's production control department. They were the seven known works rally cars, and a single chassis number (37953) which was allocated to the Development Department in 1966.

TABLE 5 Summary of total Abingdon production

	BN4	BN6	BN7 MkI	BT7 MkI	BN7 MkII	BT7 MkII	BJ7	BJ8 PhI	BJ8 PhII	Total
1957	329									329
1958	2794	3821								6615
1959	1118	329	1691	4762						7900
1960			1085	5920						7005
1961			49	143	214	3155				3561
1962					141	1941	2581			4663
1963							3532	344		3876
1964								1046	3828	4874
1965									3947	3947
1966									5495	5495
1967									3051	3051
1968									1	1
Total	4241	4150	2825	10825	355	5096	6113	1390	16322	**51317**

the series of body numbers jumped so dramatically towards the end of BJ7 production. The second series of body numbers was continued (after the break indicated) for the BJ8 models. BJ8 series production was stopped in November/ December 1967; only one car was completed in March 1968.

Table 3 attempts to date the 3000 models by their chassis numbers, with the usual warning that the first and last chassis numbers quoted for each year are only approximate. But the general picture that emerges is quite clear.

Table 4 gives the production figures for the different models, again split in the various specifications. CKD cars with RHD were for South Africa, and LHD CKD cars for Mexico. No CKD cars were made after 1961.

It will be noted that these total production figures for the Mark I, Mark II and Mark III models all match the chassis number series quoted elsewhere. For a detailed description of the 'Phase I' and 'Phase II' Mark III models please refer to 'Production Changes' and the main body of text.

Table 5 provides a clearer summary of the numbers of cars built at Abingdon, model-by-model and year-by-year.

If the previous tables have demonstrated exactly how overwhelming the number of cars made to North American export specification was (42873 cars or 83.5 per cent of the total, most shipped to the USA), table 5 also clearly shows the sudden dip in production occasioned by the collapse of the US market for import cars in late 1960 and 1961. Unfortunately there are no market-by-market export figures available.

COLOUR SCHEMES

The first table of colour schemes covers the 100-Six models, and the 3000 Mark I and II models, *except* the Mark II Convertible (BJ7).

Some early Longbridge-built 100-Six BN4 cars of 1956 were finished in the old Healey 100 colour of Reno Red rather than Colorado Red. The official hard top colours were Black, Ivory White, Healey Blue, Colorado Red and Florida Green. A few cars had hard tops in Pacific Green or Primrose Yellow. Hard tops could also be supplied in primer. Florida Green hard tops were usually not found on 3000 cars, and Red hard tops were very rare on 3000 Mark II models. A few cars had unusual hard top/ body colour combinations not covered by the table above.

The boot liners on early 100-Six BN4 cars were colour coded in blue, red, green or black to match carpet colours. All later cars had black boot liners. On the other hand, door seals were originally all black, but became colour coded Furflex to match interior trim in red, blue, black or grey on later BN4 cars, all BN6 cars and all 3000 models. On cars with yellow trim, door seals were black. The wheels were always finished in silver (Aluminium) paint.

Table 2 covers the Mark II and Mark III convertible models, types BJ7 and BJ8. Please note that on these cars a tonneau cover became an optional extra. A hard top was not offered for the convertible models. Contrast colour seat piping was found only on the Mark II. Mark III cars with Ambla trim all had piping in 'imitation chrome', while Mark III cars with the optional hide (leather) upholstery had piping in the main seat upholstery colour.

Any colour scheme involving grey upholstery/trim and hood was comparatively rare on the Mark III model, but red with grey trim and hood at least remained available to the end of

TABLE 1 BN4/BN6/BT7/BN7 colours

Paint	Upholstery and trim	Seat piping	Carpet	Hood and tonneau cover	Hard top	Notes
Black	Red	Black	Red	Black	Black, White, Red	
Ivory White	Red Black	White White	Red Black	Black Black	Black, White Black, White	
Colorado Red	Red Grey	Black Red	Red Red	Black Grey	Black, White, Red Black, White, Red	(1)
Healey Blue	Blue	White	Blue	Blue	Black, White, Blue	
Florida Green	Grey	Green	Green	Grey	White	(2)
Pacific Green	Grey	Green	Green	Grey	White, Florida Green	(3, 4)
Primrose Yellow	Black	Yellow White	Black	Black	Black	
Duotones (upper/lower paint colours)						
Ivory White/ Black	Red Black	White White	Red Black	Black Black	Black, White Black, White	
Colorado Red/ Black	Red Grey	Black Red	Black Red	Black Grey	Black, Red Black, Red	
Black/Colorado Red	Red	Black	Red	Black	Black, White, Red	
Healey Blue/ Ivory White	Blue	White	Blue	Blue	White, Blue	
Florida Green/ Ivory White	Grey	Green	Green	Grey	White, Florida Green	(2, 3)
Pacific Green/ Ivory White	Grey	Green	Green	Grey	White, Florida Green	(3)
Pacific Green/ Florida Green	Grey	Green	Green	Grey	Black, Florida Green	(3, 4)
Primrose Yellow/Black	Yellow Black	Black Yellow White	Black Black	Black Black	Black Black	(5)

Notes:

(1) Alternatively with grey hood on 100-Six models

(2) Black trim and hood on some early 100-Six models

(3) Florida Green hard tops not usually found on 3000 models

(4) This colour scheme virtually discontinued on 3000 Mark II models

(5) Some interior trim parts (normally colour coded) were black rather than yellow for this colour scheme

TABLE 2 BJ7/BJ8 Colours

Paint	Upholstery and trim	Seat piping (MkII)	Carpet	Hood and tonneau cover	Notes
Black	Red	Black	Red	Black	(6)
Ivory White	Red	White	Red	Black	
	Black	White	Black	Black	
Colorado Red	Red	Black	Red	Black	
	Grey	Red	Red	Grey	
	Black	Red	Black	Black	
Healey Blue	Blue	White	Blue	Blue	
Florida Green	Grey	Green	Green	Grey	(7)
British Racing Green	Black	Black	Black	Black	(8)
Metallic Golden Beige	Red	n/a	Red	Black	(9)
	Black	n/a	Black	Black	(9)
Duotones (upper/lower paint colours)					
Ivory White/Black	Red	White	Red	Black	(10)
	Black	White	Black	Black	
Colorado Red/Black	Red	Black	Black	Black	
	Grey	Red	Red	Grey	(11)
	Black	Red	Black	Black	(12)
Black/Colorado Red	Red	Black	Red	Black	
Healey Blue/Ivory White	Blue	White	Blue	Blue	
Florida Green/Ivory White	Grey	Green	Green	Grey	(13)

Notes:

(6) Black trim and carpet on some Mark III cars
(7) Discontinued in September 1966
(8) From the start of BJ8 production, this colour was changed to Dark British Racing Green
(9) Introduced in February 1967
(10) Discontinued in December 1966
(11) Later cars in 1965-66 had black hoods; discontinued August 1966
(12) Introduced in 1963
(13) Very rare; discontinued in September 1965

production. Two-tone colour schemes became progressively rarer towards the end of production. Metallic Golden Beige, as on the car photographed for this book, was the most unusual of the colours – only 553 cars were finished in this colour.

No attempt has been made to cover special colour orders or one-offs, but it may be mentioned that before British Racing Green was introduced as a standard colour in 1963 a few 3000 Mark I and Mark II cars were finished in this colour, apparently including the Sebring race cars. On the other hand the works rally cars were red with white hard tops. A few cars were finished in white over red. One car was metallic silver grey. Another was black over pink, with pink trim! There were probably cars supplied in primer. The CKD cars assembled in South Africa and Mexico may have been painted in special colours locally, or may have had non-standard combinations of paint/trim colours.

Table 3 covers all of the 100-Six and 3000 colours with their BMC colour codes and ICI paint manufacturer's colour numbers.

TABLE 3 Colour codes

Colour name	BMC code number	ICI code number
Aluminium (wheels)	AL.1	?
Black	BK.1	122 (?)
Metallic Golden Beige	BG.19	3006M/2496M
Healey Blue (Ice Blue Metallic)	BU.2	2697/2301M
Florida Green	GN.1	2997
Pacific Green	GN.9	2659
British Racing Green	GN.25	8120
Dark British Racing Green	GN.29	9767
Colorado (Signal) Red	RD.2	3742
Primrose (Sunburst) Yellow	YL.3	3011
Ivory (Old English) White	WT.3	2379/2122

This table also gives the alternative names used by BMC for some of these colours when used on other models of car.

Buying Guide

The only problem in buying a Big Healey is in deciding how much money you want to spend! Some cars now on the market are remarkably cheap in anyone's terms, but they are likely to be re-imports from the USA in relatively poor condition. On the other hand, if you have set your heart on a 100S or an authenticated works rally or race car, be prepared to fork out a very substantial six-figure sum . . .

With the numbers of cars coming back from the USA, do bear in mind that these are, or originally were, left-hand drive. If you are not concerned about using a LHD car on the road, don't worry. If you prefer, there are RHD conversions available – at a price, and not all of them equally satisfactory. If you are faced with what appears to be a RHD car, do check the chassis number prefix, which on all models originally built as LHD cars will have the tell-tale letter 'L' (unless given a new chassis plate).

Basically, there are three sources for buying cars: private owners, dealers or auctions. A privately-sold car may be cheaper and may have more of a known history, but you may be on your own as far as judging condition and originality is concerned. The responsible dealers should accept some liability in these matters, to avoid infringing the Trade Description Act. But obviously they may charge more to show a profit. The potentially most desirable – and expensive – cars tend to show up at auctions, and you can never be sure how high the bids will go; you may also have to pay a buyers' premium. However, some auction houses take an interest in establishing the provenance and history of the cars they accept.

For UK buyers contemplating an imported car, or wanting to buy their own Healey abroad, remember that while you can avoid paying import duty on a car originally made in Britain, and that while you do not have to pay any car tax on cars more than 20 years old, HM Customs & Excise will want their cut in the form of 15 per cent VAT – unless you can prove that the car was originally registered, tax-paid, in the UK. And unless you can produce the original log book, you have no such proof. The VAT is payable on what you have paid

for the car, abroad or in this country, and if you are buying abroad VAT will also be levied on the shipping costs and insurance while in transit. Don't try to present a Bill of Sale for $50.00 – Customs & Excise officers can read the classic car magazines as well as you can, and will happily impose their own valuation if they think it is necessary.

But what are you really looking for? One of the worst problems with the Big Healeys is inevitably corrosion. While the front shroud and rear tonneau panels are from aluminium, all other body panels are steel, and they will rust. The petrol tank rusts out on the underside. Rust may also ultimately get into the chassis itself. Some replacement body panels and part panels are available from specialists, and re-manufactured chassis for the six-cylinder cars are also coming on to the market. Do not be deceived by a flashy paint job which may cover up shoddy body repairs and filler.

One particular problem on the Big Healey is the electrolytic corrosion which may occur where aluminium panels meet steel panels – typically along the top edges of the wings. The weakest points on the chassis are the outriggers, particularly the rear ones which carry the spring shackles, and the rear crossmember. It should also be checked that the chassis is straight, rather than bent after accident damage. There is a useful dimensional diagram in the factory workshop manual for the 100-Six and 3000 models.

Mechanical components are generally robust. The four-cylinder engines may be prone to overheating, which could eventually lead to the cylinder head warping or cracking. Cracked heads are common, and replacements are difficult as no reproductions are available. There is also a fairly persistent tendency for oil leakage from the crankshaft seals front and rear. The six-cylinder engines also are generally very rugged, but the rocker shaft is prone to wear, as it is on the four-cylinder engine. If you cannot be bothered about the extra problem of balancing three carburettors, avoid the 3000 Mark II two- and four-seater models. Cooling systems and radiators have often been neglected, so the cars run too hot.

The three-speed gearbox of the early 100 BN1 model is a weak area as the second speed gears are prone to failure. Otherwise, there are no particular problems in the transmission area; even the overdrives are generally well-behaved, and rebuilds are straightforward if required. King pins usually need replacing. Wire wheels should be checked for broken or loose spokes. However, wire wheel rebuild facilities are generally available in the UK. Worn splines on wire wheels and hubs are a common and serious problem, but replacement wheels and hubs are available.

Which model of Healey to go for is a matter of personal preference. Among the four-cylinder cars, the four-speed BN2 is more sought-after, and is also rarer. A genuine factory-built 100M seems to be worth a lot more money than a standard car, or a conversion. Of the 100-Six models, the favourite is the rare two-seater BN6, which always has the six-port engine. By contrast the early BN4 cars with their four-port engines are the stepchildren of the family.

In the 3000 range, the three-carb Mark II models, especially the two-seater version, are sought after for their rarity. But most enduringly popular is the Mark III Convertible which combines the most powerful engine in any Big Healey with a more refined and civilised interior. Admittedly, this is more of a Grand Touring car than an outright sports car – such as the original 100.

In terms of usage, there is little in it. All of these are powerful cars with top speeds over 100mph. The fours are a little more economical than the sixes. On the other hand, for present and future use, a converted cylinder head is now available for the 3000 so you can use lead-free petrol. All of the Healeys steer, handle and brake equally well. They are also all of them likely to fry your feet! The problem of excessive heat in the footwells, especially on the left-hand side, was never really overcome. The other snag is the lack of ground clearance at the back. Least affected is the Mark III Phase II model. But if this is going to be a problem, perhaps you should be looking at a Land Rover rather than a Big Healey . . .

Clubs

Austin-Healey Club, c/o Mrs Carol Marks, 171 Coldharbour Road, Bristol BS6 7SX, England.
This was the original Austin-Healey Club, founded with BMC support back in the 1950s, but since 1968 run independently. Local centres are run throughout the UK. The club publishes the magazine Rev Counter. *For addresses of national or regional Austin-Healey clubs in other parts of the world not listed here, please contact this UK club in the first instance.*

Clubs in the USA
Austin-Healey Club of America Inc,
    603 E. Euclid, Arlington Heights, IL
    60004
Austin-Healey Club Pacific Centre,
    PO Box 6197, San Jose, CA 95150
Cascade Austin-Healey Club,
    PO Box 39, Lynwood, WA 98046
Austin-Healey Sports and Touring Club,
    PO Box 3539, York, PA 17402.

Specialists

The following information is believed to be correct as of early 1990. Neither the author nor the publishers will be held liable for any errors or omissions or the consequences thereof. No recommendation is implied by the inclusion of a firm in this section.

UK
A-H Spares Ltd, Unit 7, Westfield Road, Southam Industrial Estate, Southam, Warwickshire CV33 0JH. Tel: 0926 81 7181.
Parts
Austin-Healey Associates Limited, Beech Cottage, North Looe, Reigate Road, Ewell, Surrey KT17 3DH. Tel: 081-393-8831.
Parts
BK Engineering, Lindens Pool House, Aldridge Road, Streetly, Sutton Coldfield, West Midlands B74 2DP. Tel: 021-353-0378.
Parts, service, restoration
Burlen Fuel Systems Ltd, Spitfire House, Castle Road, Salisbury, Wiltshire SP1 3SA. Tel: 0722 412500.
SU carburettors and fuel pumps, parts and rebuilds
John Chatham Cars, 138 Gloucester Road, Bishopston, Bristol BS7 8NT. Tel: 0272 424154/48335.
Parts, restoration, race preparation
Classic Components, 10 Olive Street, Sunderland, Tyne & Wear. Tel: 091-510-1473.
Parts
The Don Trimming Co Ltd, Hampton Road, Erdington, Birmingham B23 7JJ. Tel: 021-373-1313.
Trim parts, carpets, hoods, etc.
Hardy Engineering, 268 Kingston Road, Leatherhead, Surrey. Tel: 0372 378927.
Transmission parts and rebuilds

Holden Vintage and Classic Spares Company, Unit 43B, Hartlebury Trading Estate, Hartlebury, Kidderminster, Worcestershire DY10 4JB. Tel: 0299 251353.
Lucas electrical parts
JME, 18 Green Farm End, Kineton, Warwickshire CV35 0LD (workshop at: 4A Wise Terrace, Leamington Spa, Warwickshire). Tel: 0926 640031/425038.
Restoration
K and J B Restorations Ltd, The Croft, Back Lane, Long Lawford, Warwickshire. Tel: 0788 78848.
Restoration
Motor Wheel Service Repair Co, 65 Jeddo Road, Shepherds Bush, London W12 9ED. Tel: 081-743-3532.
Wire wheel rebuilds
The Northern Healey Centre, Castleford, West Yorkshire. Tel: 0977 555211.
Parts and restoration
Orchard Engineering, Whatley's Garage, High Street, Horam, West Sussex. Tel: 04353 2374.
Restoration, servicing and tuning
Performance Car Services, Trinity Court, Trinity Street, Bungay, Suffolk. Tel: 0986 4480.
Restoration, servicing, race preparation
SC Austin-Healey Parts, 13 Cobham Way, Gatwick Road, Crawley, West Sussex RH10 2RX. Tel: 0293 547841-4.
Parts
Denis Welsh Motors Ltd, Sudbury Road Garage, Yoxall, Burton-on-Trent, Staffordshire DE13 8NA. Tel: 0543 472214.
Competition parts, race preparation

USA

Absolutely British II, 1720 S.Grove Ave,
Unit A, Ontario, CA 91761. Tel: 714–947-
0200.
Parts, service, restoration
The Austin-Healey Store, 8225 Remmet
Ave, Canoga Park, CA 91304. Tel: 818-
992-3234.
Parts
British Car Centre (Norman Nock), 2060
N.Wilson Way, Stockton, CA 92505.
Parts, service, restoration
British Wire Wheel, 1600 Mansfield St,
Santa Cruz, CA 95062. Tel: 408-479-4495.
Wire wheel rebuilds
Brit Parts Mid-West, 603 Monroe St,
LaPorte, IN 46350. Tel: 219-324-5474.
Six-cylinder engine parts
FASPEC British Cars & Parts, 1036SE
Stark St, Portland, OR 97214. Tel: toll-free
800-547-8788; from OR only, 503-232-
1232.
Parts
Fourintune (Tom Kovacs), W.63 N.147
Washington Ave, Cedarburg, WI 53012.
Tel: 414-375-0876.
Restoration
Healey Surgeons Inc, 7211 Carroll Ave,
Takoma Park, MD 20912. Tel: 301-270-
8811.
Parts, service, restoration
Hemphill's Healey Haven Ltd, 4–B Winters
Lane, Catonsville, MD 21228. Tel: 301-788-
2291.
Parts
Moss Motors Ltd, 7200 Hollister Ave, PO
Box MG, Goleta, CA 93116. Tel: toll-free
800-235-6954; from CA only, 800-322-
6985.
Parts
Sports and Classics Inc, 512 Boston Post
Road, Darien, CT 06820. Tel: 203-655-
8731/8732.
Parts

Sports Cars Restored, 705 Dimmeydale,
Deerfield, IL 60015. Tel: 312-945-1360.
Parts, restoration
Victoria British Ltd, Box 14991, Lenexa,
KS 66215. Tel: 913-541-8500; toll-free 800-
255-0088.
Parts
Walsh Motor Works, 25344 Little John
Lane, Pioneer, CA 95666. Tel: 209-295-
4429.
Service and restoration

Canada

The Healey Den, 1162 Seymour Street,
Vancouver, BC.

Australia

The Healey Factory, 73-79 Heatherdale
Road, Ringwood, VIC 3134. Tel: (03) 872
3900.

This list is by no means exhaustive but gives
a good cross-section of Austin-Healey
specialists. Many other firms, particularly in
the UK and the USA, offer parts and
restoration services for the Big Healeys.
Reference to other specialists will often be
found in club publications or specialist
magazines.